THE SECRETLY NAUGHTY ONE!

JENNY's our problem girl. Boy, has she got problems. About 200 of them on her desk every morning—and every one's important. Greg helps with the boys' letters and tries to get his legs under her desk as they sit together, but she copes with him very well. And then at office parties there she is with a wicked twinkle in her eye and she's dynamite! Called 'Little Miss Mouse' at first, she's now known to several envious female mates as 'Super Rat'! She has no problems with fellas, she says—must be reading all their letters. She knows their weak-spots only too well!

THE SCATTERBRAIN!

LIZ, our fashion brain, beauty brain, and scatterbrain . . . what can we say, but . . . HELP! She'll lose her desk one day, an entire circus and big top the next . . . . it's not possible, but she does! It may be something to do with her office. When she can find it, it looks like a boutique gone berserk! And yet she manages to stay looking cucumber cool and marvellous. Every time she comes in we're deafened by the sound of Jenny and Nicki's grinding teeth!

£1·45

3

PART 1

OH BOY! THEY'RE BEAUTIFUL!

Nothing but the best—nothing but the most beautiful—you know you can rely on Oh Boy! to give you the best pics of the best-looking fellas around.

So how about these for starters? And if you turn to pages 86 and 87 you'll find five more gorgeous hunks captured by the Oh Boy! cameras!

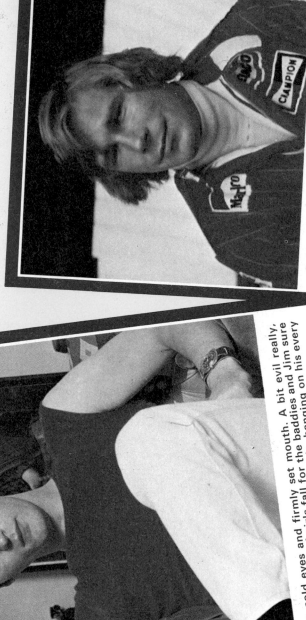

Quite a hero, James Hunt, but he doesn't look big-headed at all. He needs determination for motor racing and you can see it in his eyes. You'd know he was the boss alright, no messin' with him. Just a little bit untidy an' that makes you wanna look after him. Darn his socks an' polish his trophies.

Mean-looking, that Jim McGinlay. Ice cold eyes and firmly set mouth. A bit evil really, but that's what makes him. Lots of girls fall for the baddies and Jim sure hardly ever smiles but the sharp snap of his fingers and you'd be there at his side, hanging on his every looks like one. Sharp snap of his fingers and you'd be there at his side, hanging on his every word. Even Dennis Waterman'd have trouble saving you from his grasp!

He's chirpy, Alan Richardson, and looks sincere. Wouldn't hurt a fly but doesn't want to be taken for a fool. Wise inside and someone you could lean on when things get you down. Always aware but not loud unless asked for his opinion. Then he's good to listen to. Beautiful 'cos he's nice all the way through.

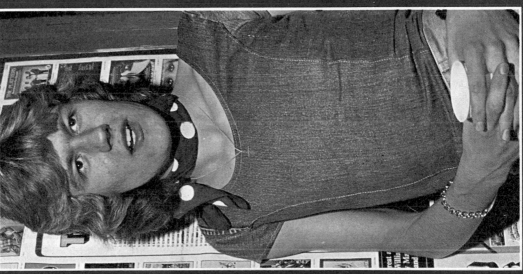

Dead sexy is Graham Bilborough. He's the really cool lookin' Child. He's got people worked out. Knows where he's going and you can go along for the ride if you want. Makes you want to have a try at meltin' his heart.

Peter Frampton is beautiful and bubbly. Laughs a lot and enjoys life. When he was younger he used to be a bit too pretty, a touch too perfect. Now he's a little more ragged but just as handsome. Good cheek bones and strong features. Dresses with a gypsy touch. Full of life.

THE NIGHT THE DIDN'T MAKE IT...

Our Steve has shared one of the Rollers' most petrifying moments. When he went to interview them one evening at their hotel, someone phoned with a terrible message . . .

THE ROLLERS are always in a bit of a muddle before they do a show. I knocked on their hotel room door and Woody answered, his hair soaking wet and nothing on except a towel. He gave me a big grin and dragged me inside muttering something about someone knicking his shampoo.

I got out my notebook and looked around at the mess. There were socks sticking out of drawers and shirts crumpled on the floor. Leslie was the only one sitting still

so I started to ask him about how their recording had been going. He was very enthusiastic and happy.

Suddenly the phone rang and Les leaned across to answer it. "That'll be room service," he told me. "I've ordered scampi and chips an' it should be ready." With his ear to the receiver, he listened for a few seconds and then began to look very pale and shaky. "Okay, okay, anything you say," he murmered and hung

up.

Everyone had noticed how frightened he looked and we all waited for him to speak.

"It's Tam," he told us with a trembling voice. "He's been kidnapped."

We all just looked at each other. As far as we knew Tam was on his way from Edinburgh and should've been arriving at any minute.

"What'll we do?" Woody asked. "Are they after money or what?"

"Yes," Les nodded. "We've got to take them £10,000. It was a woman who called, her voice was very muffled. We'll have to cancel the concert and try to get the cash somehow . . ."

"Don't be stupid," Eric butted in. "Cancel the show, sure we're forced to, but call the police. We can't handle this on our own."

"But they say they'll kill him," Les whispered. "For all we know, he's already dead."

ROLLERS NEARLY

"Now don't panic," Eric said, taking charge of things. This is probably just a joke or something anyway. Don't get all morbid. Where do they want us to go?"

"To a wood," Les explained. "All of us!"

Eric picked up the phone and began to dial. Just as he got through to the police, Tam walked through the door, ghost-like in his white suit.

"I got a flat tyre," he began to tell us but before he could say anymore, the Rollers all cheered loudly with relief and Eric explained what had happened.

"You daft lot," Tam scolded with mock anger, "as if anyone could have nobbled me! Some of your fans are pretty clever, y'know. That was probably just a girl trying to get to meet you. They're always trying to scare me. Last week one lass reckoned she'd got my mum and wanted Eric as the ransom!"

We all felt a bit silly at falling for the trick but I could tell the Rollers were really glad that Tam was safe. And the show went on after all . . .

Les nearly didn't get to thrill the fans that night!

The Rollers never know if a call is genuine, or a hoax . . .

IT'S SMOULDERIN' STARSKY!

Who's the loveliest supercop of 'em all? It's P.M.G. — the Prettiest, Meanest Guy on the baddy trail!

ONE MINUTE it was just another American detective series, and the next the whole of Britain was talking about it.

Starsky and Hutch took us all by storm, there's no doubt about it.

And the Supercop who kept edging forward in popularity was Paul Michael Supersexy. Well, that's what we knew him as. To his doctor he was filed G for Glaser.

And the Glaser Phase isn't over yet. There's something about Starsky that makes a fan stay a fan—through thick and thin. Through odd little crushes on the latest pop superstar and flirtations with Dr Who, Kojak, or Ironside (well, perhaps not Ironside, but you know what we mean . . .)

Girls all over the world keep coming back to smoulderin' Starsky. The dark eyes, the face that looks lived-in, knocked-around and just plain gorgeous—his looks are different, yes, but they're not all there is to Starsky.

MOODY

He's happy-go-lucky, and tough. He's mean, moody, and as gentle as can be. He's . . . well, he's just Starsky.

"Sometimes I wonder what it's all about, this fan thing," he says. "I mean—is it me the ladies like, or is it that cop they see on the TV running all over the place and making things tough for the hoods?"

The answer's simple, Stars. It's both you and your telly image we love. Cos you couldn't be one without the other—you're linked now in our hearts. And you'll take some budging.

They say that some partnerships are made in heaven. Woody and Eric. Simon and Garfunkel. George and Mildred—well, just a little bit— and Starsky and Hutch. They work perfectly on the set, and they're good mates off, too.

They love to eat together in some backstreet Hollywood cafe where they can relax and just be themselves. But sometimes they can't even do that...

DRUNK

"I remember one night very clearly," Paul smiled. "We were just deciding on what to eat when a big drunk guy about the size of a fire station comes up to us. " 'You think you're tough, huh?' " he said to David.

" 'Nope,' said David. 'Well, you're dead right there' replied the big guy and bopped him so hard on the jaw I swear I heard the bones crunch. David went out like a light bulb, and stayed out too.

" 'An' you mister, you're the one my goddam daughter's nuts about . . . I'm gonna rip you apart!' He lunged at me with a chair and I felt it whistle over my head and crash into a mirror above the bar It was just like one of those Wild West punch-ups!

"I squared up to him and while he was trying to get his balance I socked him so hard my hand went black with bruising. He sort of swayed a little, then righted himself and grinned.

CRASH

" 'Say goodbye to God's earth, son!' he rasped through some horrible broken teeth. And just as I was about to do just that, his eyes went all glassy and he fell with an enormous crash onto the table— nearly poking his eye out on the tomato sauce bottle!

"Whew—was that a night! Suddenly I was sitting at a table with two unconscious guys! It really put me off my meal!"

That's Starsky for you—we never could tell if he was joking or not about that story.

But we can just picture him sitting there with Hutch out, and the drunk sprawled across him like a huge felled tree.

We bet he just sat there, grinning at the waitress, leaning back on his chair with his legs on the table, and doing with his eyes what he just can't help doing . . .

Smoulderin' . . .

D'YOU LET BOYS

Are you a lily-livered pushover when it comes to fellas or do you give 'em *more* than they bargained for? Better do our quiz and find out...

1. You're at the local flics with your mate, both deeply engrossed in the deep, blue pools of Robert Redford's eyes when you feel this hot sweaty mitt on your kneecap! Do you:
a) Put up with it until the interval and then change seats.
b) Punch him on the hooter then go and get the manager to have him thrown out.
c) Drop your choc-ice in his lap and hope *that* cools his ardour!

2 You've been waiting for ages in the pouring rain for a bus and when it *does* come this fella tries to barge in front of you in the queue. Do you:
a) Give way to his superior strength and hope you get on before the bus is full.
b) Kick him sharply on the ankle, poking him at the same time with the specially sharpened point of your brolly and jump on to the bus, leaving him writhing in agony in a puddle.
c) Shout, "Hey, isn't that Lynsey de Paul over there?" and nip smartly on to the platform while he's not looking!

3 You're sitting in the local Wimpy mindin' your own business and sippin' your frothy milk-shake when this clumsy great oaf knocks into you, making a soggy banana mess of your new Slik T-shirt. Do you:
a) Burst into floods of tears while he paws at your front with his man-sized Kleenex.
b) Squirt the tomato sauce in his stupid face and scoot while he's incapacitated!
c) Rip off the offending article and force him to give you that super baseball shirt he's wearing to cover your shame!

4 You fancy a bop down the disco but your fella fancies the flics (Well Ursula Andress actually!). Would you:
a) Insist you both go to the disco or go on your own.
b) Go to the pictures anyway cos you hate arguments.
c) Agree to go to the flics with him (as long as it's that James Dean film they're showing at the Roxy that is!).

5 You're down the disco strutting your stuff when suddenly you feel this hot, sweaty paw on your left cheek (not the one under your left eye either!). Do you:
a) Turn round, look him in the eye and knee him right where it'll make his eyes water!
b) Put your hand over his, grab his other hand and launch into a tango!
c) Pretend you haven't noticed and do your best to shake him off with your sexy wiggle.

6 You've met this fella at a party and he's giving you a lift home when (surprise, surprise) the car 'breaks down' in a dark secluded spot. He looks at you—an evil glint in his eye. Do you:
a) Jump out of the car shouting red, white and blue murder and searching in your handbag for your police whistle.
b) Say, "O well, let's get the bonnet up then. I knew those car maintenance classes 'd come in useful sometime".
c) Stay put and hope it doesn't take *too* long (to fix that is!).

7 You're sprawled out on the beach in your itsy-bitsy when along comes this shark on two legs, looking like he'd like to get his hands on more than your beachball. Do you:
a) Fix him with an icy stare so's he wishes he was somewhere warmer—like the North Pole for instance!
b) Go for a swim and risk the real sharks.
c) Offer him one of your sardine butties cos he looks a bit hungry.

8 You arrange to meet your boyfriend outside the disco at 7.30 and he turns up at 8.00 with the excuse he forgot what time he was supposed to meet you! It's not the first time either. Do you:
a) Act a bit grumpy but be thankful he turned up at all.
b) Attempt to tie a knot in his neck so he won't have any excuse for forgetting in future!
c) Tell him not to worry cos it gave you plenty of time to eye up the talent!

9 Your fella starts getting heavy cos he feels you see too much of your mates and not enough of him. Do you:
a) Feel flattered and see him as often as he likes.
b) Tell him it's not your fault you're so popular but he's quite welcome to come along sometimes when you go out with your mates!
c) Think, O he's being heavy is he? Well, drop him like a ton of cowpat!

10 You're just settling down for a cosy trio with the telly (you, Starsky 'n' Hutch) when in he comes reeking of sweat and demanding you switch over and watch the footy on Colenight with Sportsman or whatever it is. Do you:
a) Show him a bit of nifty footwork yourself (with a flying drop kick in the penalty area!).
b) Decide you're really interested in the fifth round of the cup too, and offer him a cup of cocoa to spill all over the carpet in his excitement.
c) Switch over and drool over 44 hairy knees (46 counting the ref!).

MUSCLE IN ON YOU?

SCORES

	a)		b)		c)			a)		b)		c)	
1		0		10		5	**6**		10		5		0
2		0		10		5	**7**		10		5		0
3		0		10		5	**8**		0		10		5
4		10		0		5	**9**		0		5		10
5		10		5		0	**10**		10		0		5

0-35) Talk about a pushover-you never stood up in your life! You're so weak we're surprised you managed to get this far without breaking out in a rash and running to mum! Fellas probably reckon you're sweet tho'—but remember, too much sugar ain't healthy!

40-65) You give a bit, take a bit depending on your mood, on the fella you're with at the time and whether there's an R in the month! Basically you're pretty fun to be with-unless you've got a stroppy boyfriend. Then you put your foot down hard—on his toes!

70-100) Wow! Better stay outa your way! You're the original Tough Cookie. When fellas snap their fingers you snap their legs— and then you step in and give 'em some REAL punishment. Don't be too tough, cookie— we reckon you just might end up like a dinosaur with bad breath. Dead lonely.

IT'S WELLIE-WEATHER!

Get swoppin' those cosy sweaters for a pair o' gleamin' wellies! An' be the best puddle-splasher around

WE KNOW you've been sneakily hidin' under your thick woollies an' leg warmers all winter—but now all will be revealed! An' anyone with a spare tyre an' podgey knees— get slimming! Cos summer's just around the corner, an' we don't wanna see thousands of fatties lying around in bikinis, do we?

1.
When you're as slim as this, you know you've won!

CUT IT OUT!

Cut down on the amount you're eating. An' it's no good sayin' you don't eat that much, cos we won't believe ya! Get your mum to put your dinner on a smaller plate, then it won't look so drastic!

Cut out all snacks between meals, it's no good chompin' on crisps an' Mars bars then wonderin' why you're puttin' on weight! If you feel like a nibble, grab hold of your fella!

USE YOUR NUT!

There are oodles of diets, so have a scout around to see if one of 'em will suit you. Tho' keep off the crash diets! A lettuce leaf a day may taste alright, but you'll soon get weak an' unhealthy! Just use your nut! Cut out all carbohydrates like bread an' potatoes, an' sweet sugary deserts like tarts, puddings, cakes an' biscuits. See if that helps. If it does, carry on. If not, try another!

Tuck into the fresh veg, cos it contains vitamins that you'll need. Cabbage an' spinach are 'specially good for you (an' y'know what it did for Popeye!). Fresh fruit is a good substitute for desserts—try chopped strawberries with yoghurt yummm. . .! Or make your own!

STICK IT OUT!

Just keep to it! Even if you don't lose anything in the first couple of weeks, you will later, so be patient. Do a few exercises each

2.
If rosy cheeks don't come naturally, add lotsa blusher!

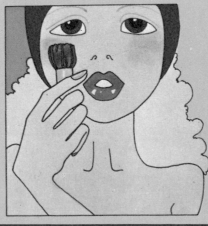

3.
Are you eatin' plenty of fruit? It's great for your skin!

day. No—we don't mean going for a mile jog an' doing twenty press-ups before breakfast, stupid! Just do, say, ten touch-your-toes before you go to bed, that'll be enough. It helps to tone up the figure in the places that you were once fat!

Don't forget to take care of your skin, when you're concentrating on your body! Tho' if you are eatin' loads of fresh fruit an' veg, it should be better than before. Clearing your spots up to boot!

Get a lotta fresh air—in the rain if possible—cos there'll be enough around! A day rompin' about in that, and you'll have the biggest, rosiest cheeks ever! If that doesn't help, never mind, brush on loads of blusher. That'll do the trick! Cheat!

CAUGHT UNAWARES!

Well, are ya all kitted out? No good venturing out into puddle-land without the right gear! First essential —wellies! Then a rain-mac and umbrella. Me, Jenny an' Nicki were all out the other day, when, one minute there was a bright sky, then the next it was black! An' it started to bucket down! Caught us unawares, didn't it! An' not an umbrella 'tween us! Wonder what that ol' man at the bus stop was starin' at? It couldn't have been the sight of us, three drowned rats sittin' on the pavement with plastic cement bag over our heads, could it?!!

NOTHIN' LIKE A WELLIE!

Hope your wellies are in prime nick to last the spring. Betcha didn't know that our Greg was a wellie-wotsit, didya? Doesn't take 'em off, y'know! We were only sayin' a while ago that his 'doodles' had had their day (that's what he calls his wellies, cos he draws silly faces on 'em). Well, that started it! We had to go thro' the tale of how he wears 'em in the shower to keep his feet dry, an' how, on cold nights, he tucks up with his hot wellie-bottle! At a party not long ago, to celebrate Nicki's retirement (!!) he turned off the music an' announced he was goin' to make a toast. Cor,

champers all round, we thought! Then the pig whipped one of his wellies off an' filled it wiv beer! An' he expected us all to have a sip! "Well, this is to celebrate . . . he began, the 20th season of me beloved doodles, cos I've proved they don't leak!!" Hah, some toast! A bit wellie-brained if ya ask me!

THE SEXY ONE AND THE SCATTERBRAIN!

Well, it all started one cold grey November day . . .

We'd just started the magazine up—I think we were on issue four—and everyone was dead excited about it.

Spanking new desks, new faces—and that day we heard that we had quite a few readers too.

And best news of all—one of 'em (the little beauty) had christened me "the sexy one".

When I opened the letter Liz was the only other one in the office.

"Here—this'll take that daft grin off Greg's mush," I was just saying, and then I sort of fell against her.

It was an accident—honest. We clung to each other to stay upright, but ended up giggling on the floor like a couple of dummies.

That's when Nicki walked in.

"Oooh—sorry!" she said, with a big smile on her face. "I didn't know you two were, well, er—you know."

"Well—there's no law against two staff members falling desperately in love and having a quick chat on the carpet, is there?" said I, as a joke.

But Nicki didn't take it as a joke. She wanted there to be an Office Romance. The nearest she'd got to it before was getting Greg a blind

date with the tea lady—and she was never forgiven for that. By the tea lady.

With a big wink and a smile she went out again. And we heard her break into a run as she went sprinting off to find Jenny and Greg.

Well, Liz and I found it such a giggle we kept it going.

We went everywhere hand in hand and wrote love poems on each other's typewriter which everyone could 'find'.

But then things went too far. Liz announced we were getting engaged and she hoped we'd get a pressy, cos engaged couples always did.

There was a collection when they thought we

weren't looking. Bless 'em, I thought, they really care.

And then one Friday I found a big parcel on my desk—sent to "the lovers".

And in it . . . was one of the most AWFUL sights I'd ever seen. A pair of Greg's plimsolls—aged about 82½. Not smelling like roses.

Liz and I bolted for the door in blind panic and were ill for weeks.

They never miss a trick, that lot. Specially Nicki. She'd been setting us up for that one for weeks—a fiendish double cross!

And it didn't half hurt my friendship with Liz—whenever I look at her now I think of Greg's feet ! ! !

FANTASTIC – A FOUR COURSE BANQUET!

ONLY ONE THING MISSING, AND I CAN FIX THAT IN NO TIME!

LAMP-LIGHT AND FLOWERS . . . HOW'S THAT?

GORGEOUS! THOUGH I DON'T OFTEN GO TO THESE POSH RESTAURANTS.

After the snack.

THAT WAS DELICIOUS!

SO ARE YOU – AND TO ROUND OFF OUR FIRST DATE . . .

HOW ABOUT A KISS?

WHAT IS IT ABOUT RAILWAY STATIONS THAT TURNS 'EM ON LIKE THIS?

SOME OTHER TIME, MAYBE – RIGHT NOW I'D BETTER GET BACK TO MY LUGGAGE.

OKAY – I'LL COME WITH YOU!

18

19

I ALWAYS GOT WHAT I WANTED!

Name Karen Williams

Age 16 Birthplace North Lancs.

Karen wanted Steve. Karen got Steve.
But then the trouble began...

I s'pose some people would call me **lucky. Others might use a word I don't like very much—spoilt. And they could be right.**

Y'see, ever since I was a little kid, I seemed to have got just what I wanted. Sometimes I had to fight for it, but if I'd set my heart on having it, no matter what it was, I'd get it in the end. The trouble was that the more impossible it was to have something, the more I wanted it. And then, when I did finally get it, I somehow didn't want it any more.

Then one day my best mate Julia met Steve.

I couldn't believe it when I saw him. He was so good looking, like a pop star or something. Julia was nuts over him, and talked about nothing else. I didn't see why he was going out with her, I mean she's pretty, and all that, but her figure's a bit, well, y'know, underdeveloped. Whereas I'm the sort that fellas go for—I've got long blonde hair, a pretty shapely body, and a better face than Julia.

After I'd seen Steve with Julia I knew that I wanted him. Worse than that, I just had to have him for my boyfriend and to hell with Julia or anyone else who got in the way. I know it sounds terrible but I started sorta plotting how I could get Steve away from her. Y'see I just couldn't sleep for thinking about him, an' I was off my food too. Mum said, "You must be in love," and I thought she was right.

Anyway if I knew Julia was meeting Steve at the youth club at eight, I'd get there ten minutes before her, so's I could get him to myself. He always said, "Hello, gorgeous" to me as a sorta joke, but somewhere deep down I thought he might mean it, just a bit. But I could see he was gonna be difficult to get because he kept going on about Julia and how great she was. It made me want to scream when he did that, it really did!

But there was one thing I knew about Julia which gave me a bit of hope. She told me Steve had a touch of the old wandering hand trouble, y'know, he couldn't keep them to himself. And Julia, well she's the sort who doesn't like that kinda thing, I mean, she'll snog away all night, but she won't let a fella get any closer than that.

And that helped me, 'cos if a fella wants a bit of a cuddle, that's okay by me. Don't get me wrong, I'm not the sort who lets anyone mess around with me, but a little cuddling's all right.

Well, one night Julia had a cold. So she asked me if I'd mind dropping in to the youth club and telling Steve she couldn't see him that night. Me,

I just had to have Steve — and I got him.

mind seeing Steve? If only she knew!

Well, I put on a low cut dress and spent ages doing my face. If I was gonna get Steve, tonight was the night.

At the club I went straight up to him and told him about Julia not being able to come. "Perhaps I can make up for it," I said and he laughed and said, "Maybe you can."

I guess I led him on quite a bit and he put his arm round me. I just snuggled up closer to him. We didn't talk much, but I noticed his eyes kept wandering down the front of my dress with the kinda look that said his hands wanted to follow.

In the end he suggested going for a drive in his car. I knew just what he had in mind—so I said "Yes".

It wasn't a very long drive and

soon we were in a quiet little lane well away from the main road. Steve put his arm round me and kissed me . . . it was great.

And then the whole thing went wrong. I just grabbed Steve's hand and told him to stop. He said "What's the matter, I thought you liked me." So I said, "Yes, and I thought you liked Julia," and he mumbled something about Julia not being here and anyway he wasn't married to her, was he?

And then we sat in silence for what must've been ages. Y'see I was thinking about myself, and taking a good look at myself. And it wasn't very nice. I'd been a right little bitch to Julia, anyone could see that. But for what? Cos when I thought about it, what did I want Steve for?

I mean, really I'd had a pretty boring evening with him—he just wasn't very exciting. And I didn't 'specially want a guy who went off with the first girl with a bigger bust who came along. And I realised that all that time I'd been wanting him I'd never even thought about what he would be like to go out with. I just thought about getting him.

I got him to drive me home. And I said, "I'll tell Julia you'll go round and see her tomorrow," and slammed the car door behind me.

Luckily nobody's told Julia about me and Steve being together, so we're still mates. But I did get something out of that night.

I know now that you shouldn't fight for things that aren't yours, whether it's boys or anything. And before you want something, you have to be dead sure that what you want is worth having.

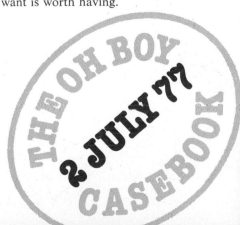

THE OH BOY
2 JULY 77
CASEBOOK

23

24

25

26

THE SECRETS OF

Revealed at last—those intimate thoughts that flash through his mind as he tries to find some socks without holes in them . . .

Have you ever thought, as you sweat away, getting yourself beautiful for a first date with a new boy, worrying over the disaster nature gave you when all you wanted was a face, have you ever wondered about him?

What's he doing? Does he bother getting ready? Does he shuffle out of the house, sniffing, and wearing the same sweaty socks and shirt he's had on all day—all week?

Or does he ponce about waving pink powder puffs and swooning because he hasn't got enough time to pluck his eyebrows?

Well, let's tiptoe into his house and see . . .

Splashings and whistlings from his loo. He washes his hair, sprinkles a few warm drops of water under his armpits. Curses his Mum for not buying his favourite herbal shampoo. Then eases a careful razor round the pimples on his face.

Stares glumly at his reflection wondering if it would take weeks to grow a moustache or a beard, and if he'd suit it. And would you fancy him more? A spot of stingy aftershave—sharp intake of breath—oooh!

He'll look down morosely at his body, flex his biceps, think how he'd be a whizz with the ladies if they were huge. Too late to start developing them to show 'em to you though. So it's on with his best shirt. With a sigh . . .

THE JOKES

What's round and pink and drives men crazy at Easter time, he thinks. A hot cross bum. Ha ha. Yeah—that'll be a swift joke to impress you. He grins in the mirror. Going through his routine. Practising his patter.

Who sits on a wall saying play it again Sham: Humpty Bogart. Another swift joke, too subtle, perhaps . . . Who're incredibly thin and go squeak squeak squeak all the way home: the three little Twiggies. Oh yes, you'd like that.

What sits on top of sky scraper buildings, swatting aeroplanes, singing boo boo bah boo; Bing Kong. Ho, ho, he thinks, a few more like that, sickening grin, and you'll be his for the taking.

BOY BEAUTIFUL!

THE 'SMALLS'

It's the underpant kid! Rummaging through his drawer looking for a suitable pair for the evening's doings. Wondering will he, won't he get to grips? Just a little, why not. And what about flame red Marks 'n' Sparks best? The Y-fronts all the best young men wear. Or perhaps the tiger-skin ones he got from a dark boutique up a dirty alley. But they're a bit worn . . .

Finds a pair of plain navy ones. Remembers an article in a magazine he read at the dentist's once. Said nice girls don't let boys do ANYTHING till at least the third date. Wonders if perhaps then plain sober navy underpants would show what a decent well-intentioned chap he is underneath the heavy breathing and persistent hands.

Thinks how absurd magazine article was anyway, seethes. Discards navy underpants, flame red will do the trick. Trousers. And he's almost ready.

THE LUCKY IRISH PENNY

Finds one pair of holeless socks. Reviews his cash situation. Where'll he take you? A disco. A bit noisy for getting to know you, and you won't hear the jokes so well.

What's on at the pictures? Not bad there for cuddling and getting close to you, also shouldn't leave him cashless all week.

One wallet. Loose change. Keys. Grubby handky. Oh, he forgot. Stops filling pockets and returns to loo. Swift splashings of cologne. Here, there and · there again. Back to finish filling his pockets with the trash he carries everywhere including his lucky Irish penny (for luck).

Unwraps a stick of chewing gum. On with the jacket. And thinking how he's looking forward to seeing you, he steps out into the night.

Rob had promised to return to her...
TILL YOU COME BACK AGAIN

There was a faint mist over the glen, and the smell of the heather was sweet. Morag lay on her stomach beside the small stream and trailed her hand in the water, watching the ripples spread.

Memories stirred in her mind. Memories of the last time she had lain here like this beside the stream . . .

It had been a fine summer day in that Year of Our Lord 1745 and Morag was trying to catch a trout to take back to the croft for supper. She lay on her belly beside the stream with her arm plunged in almost to the shoulder, and gently searched below the bank with her fingers. That was where the biggest fish were always to be found.

After a moment her hand touched the silky smoothness of a large trout. She waited, tickling its belly gently with her fingers, the way she had been taught. And then her hand closed around the fish and she swept it up onto the bank with a happy laugh. There would be a good supper for her mother and herself this night.

"Well, Morag. I see you haven't forgotten everything I taught you," said a voice behind her. "That was a very pretty piece of work."

Morag jumped to her feet, smoothing down the skirt of her long homespun dress. She looked with some resentment at the tall young Highlander who stood there, his hands on his hips, his dark eyes laughing at her.

"You'll get yourself into trouble some day, Rob McLean. Creeping up behind folk like that. How long have you been watching me?"

"Long enough. And it was pretty to see." He smiled at her, teasingly. "Surely you haven't forgotten it was myself who taught you to catch fish like that. When the two of us were nothing but bairns."

"I haven't forgotten," Morag said. Then, as something occurred to her, she turned away from him. "But I'm not talking to you, Rob McLean."

"Oh? And why not, may I ask?"

Morag laughed bitterly. As if he didn't know!

"I heard about what you were up to last night. Kissing Mary McGregor! And I'll thank you not to deny it."

WILD

"Is that all?" Rob threw back his head and laughed, tall and resplendent in his tartan plaid, his long dark hair curling about his neck. "It wasn't my fault, Morag. The lass near threw herself into my arms. What else could I do but kiss her?"

"You could have tried pushing her away!" she said acidly.

"Ah now, that wouldn't have been polite, would it?" Rob laughed. "But it meant nothing, Morag. Truly it didn't".

"No. It never does when you kiss the lasses, does it? Not—not even me."

He put his arms round her and held her close to him, tilting her face up to make her look into his eyes.

"That isn't so, Morag. You know I love you."

But did she know it? Morag wasn't sure.

Rob was so wild, that was the trouble. Everybody said so. And didn't he sometimes go raiding cattle over the border?

How could she know if he was speaking the truth when he said he loved her?

"Why did you want to see me today, Rob?" she asked suddenly.

"To tell you my news. I have to go away for a while, my bonny lass. I have to leave you."

Morag stared at him, startled, no longer caring about Mary McGregor and whether or not Rob had kissed her.

"What do you mean, go away? Where?"

"To fight." Rob's eyes were sparkling with a wild excitement. "The word is all over the glens. Prince Charlie's landed from

France and he's raising a Jacobite army to fight for the cause. I go tonight to join them."

TOO YOUNG

Morag broke free from his arms and stared at him, disbelievingly, her heart pounding like a wild bird.

"You—you're going to war? But you can't, Rob!"

"Can't I now? And why not?"

Morag shook her head blindly, feeling a great fear rising inside her. "You're no older than me, Rob. You—you're too young to go to a battle."

"Ah, but you know what's said don't you?" Rob's eyes were twinkling. "If you're old enough to kiss the lasses, you're old enough to hold a claymore. And we both know about me and the lasses . . ."

As he said this he pulled her close to him, and his lips came down on her own. For a moment Morag clung to him, lost in the sweetness of his kiss. Then a sudden anger sparked in her and she pushed him away.

"No! I—I won't listen to you. You don't love me, Rob McLean!"

"But I do, lass . . ."

Morag dashed tears from her eyes. "How can you say that—and at the same time talk of going off to leave me? If you really loved me you'd stay here. You wouldn't go away . . ."

NO GOOD

Blindly she turned and ran from him. She heard Rob's voice calling to her to come back, but she didn't heed.

"You don't love me!" she cried, over and over. "You don't love me!"

When Morag got back to the croft she found her mother cooking bannock over the open fire, a dry mixture of oatmeal and salt. It had been a hard year for the people of the Highlands, and food was scarce.

"Where have you been, lass?" her mother asked quickly, a worried look on her lined face.

Morag held up the gleaming, silvery trout. "Getting our supper."

"Oh." Her mother wiped her hands on her coarse woollen apron. "I was afraid you might have been with that Rob McLean again."

Morag shook her head, silently.

"You stay away from him, lass. He's a wild one, that boy. He'll come to no good."

Yes, Morag thought, perhaps it was true. Wild Rob. Reckless Rob. The only boy she had ever loved or wanted.

And now he was talking of going away from her!

Well, if he did he wouldn't find her waiting for him when he came back. Let him give all his kisses to Mary McGregor from now on. See if she cared!

Morag ate her supper quickly and miserably, and went to bed early. But somehow sleep wouldn't come. Thoughts of Rob's laughing face filled her mind. By now he would already be on his way to join Prince Charlie's army.

She was still lying awake when something rattled lightly against the wooden shutter that served for her window. After a second the sound came again. Somebody was throwing pebbles to attract her attention.

SERIOUS

Morag slipped quickly out of bed and opened the wooden shutter. In the darkness outside she could recognise Rob's tall figure, and a feeling of relief swept over her.

"Shhh!" She put her finger to her lips and called down to him softly. "Don't make so much noise with those pebbles. You'll wake my mother!"

"I have to talk to you, Morag!" His voice sounded deep and serious.

Morag put a shawl around her shoulders and hurried outside, taking care not to disturb her mother. The night air was cold, but she scarcely noticed it as she threw herself into Rob's arms and kissed him.

FOREVER

"Oh Rob. I knew you'd change your mind. I knew you wouldn't go away and leave me!"

"Is that what you think I've come to tell you, Morag?"

He stepped back from her, his eyes serious. It was only then Morag saw that he wore his claymore at his side, and on his back hung a round shield of thick hide.

"You—you're going?" she whispered.

"I must, my love. I go now to join the Jacobite army. But I had to see you again first. I couldn't leave with harsh words between us."

Morag felt the chill of the night now, all around her and all around the glen. She drew her shawl closer to her.

"Why have you come, Rob?"

"To tell you I'll come back to you. And to ask you to wait for me."

He took her in his arms and looked down at her.

"I love you, Morag. Do you love me?"

She willed herself to say no, but she knew that she couldn't.

"Yes, Rob. I love you."

"And you'll wait for me?"

There were tears in Morag's eyes as she said, "Forever, my love."

Rob kissed her gently. "Then we won't really be parted. I'll carry your love into battle with me. And my love will stay here with you."

"Rob . . ."

He touched her lips with his finger, to silence her. "I'll come back to you, Morag. Wait for me."

The glen seemed cold and empty as he started to walk away—young, wild Rob, tall and straight and proud.

Morag stood beside the croft, watching till he was almost out of sight, and heard the sound of his voice calling back to her through the darkness.

PROMISED

"Wait for me, Morag. I'll come back . . . I'll come back to you. . . ."

And now once again, these many months later, Morag lay beside the stream, watching the ripples, alone with her thoughts of Rob.

Much had happened since that night long ago. A battle had been fought and lost at a place called Culloden and many good men had died.

But Rob had promised he would return to her, and return he had. She could still see his laughing face in the ripples of the stream. His voice still called to her in the wind that blew through the glens.

But though she waited a thousand years she knew she would never see her wild Rob again.

WADDIYA WANNA MAKE

Who's a proper little flirty-pants then? Or are you so cool, fellas think you've climbed straight out of the freezer? Do our quiz and see . . .

1 You've just spent two hours trying to convince yourself the party ain't Dragsville, when this gorgeous man strolls in, and starts eyeing up the talent . . .
Do you—

(a) Drape yourself over the back of the sofa (hoping he'll notice you before it falls over), gaze at him under hooded lids, your glossy lips pursed in a permanent kiss?

(b) Groove energetically, without a single eyelash flutter in his direction—but pretty sure he's seen your bum wiggling its way round the room?

(c) Act little-girl-lost on a chair in the corner?

2 You're out on the town with your best mate, when suddenly you see this fella you've fancied for ages, standing outside the Odeon with *his* mate. It's time for action—so, do you—

THOSE EYES AT ME FOR...?

(a) Have hysterical giggles, trip over your jeans and cling onto your mate's arm like she's your Siamese twin.

(b) Undo yet another button of your shirt, stroll past them into the cinema, saying loudly: "I hear they still have double seats on the back row . . ."

(c) Chests out, noses in the air, you move in, cool but slow.

3 You're walking past a building site, and half a dozen tasty fellas down tools to shout, "Give us a kiss, darlin'!" Do you—

(a) Pull your anorak hood up over your head, and stare grimly at the ground.

(b) Say "How's about it, baby!" and walk past, winking over your shoulder.

(c) Turn your nose up so high, you fall into the hole they've just been digging!

4 Down at the disco, you dance with the same fella for half an hour, gazing deep into his eyes. When he says "We could make music together," do you—

(a) Say "Sure, sweetheart—but Daddy'll be here soon to pick me up after his karate class."

(b) Sigh and say— "Trouble is we don't harmonise."

(c) Give him a big wet kiss on the cheek— and then rush off to catch the last bus home.

5 You're lying on the beach, five yards away from that lovely tanned lifeguard. Do you—

(a) Balance your bikini top on the tips of your boobs — and wait.

(b) Send burning looks over the top of your "Oh Boy!", drawing him to you with your eyes.

(c) Dress to kill (all attraction, that is) in sun-hat, dark glasses and a pair of wellies in case you want to go paddling.

6 You've smiled at that fella at the bus-stop for ages. When he finally gets round to asking you out, do you—

(a) Say "Great—there's this little restaurant I know : . ."

(b) Say "Trouble is, my my boy-friend's the possessive kind."

(c) Smile and say mysteriously you'd rather go on meeting like this—bus-stops are so romantic.

35

38

GREG'S 20 WORST-EVER JOKES!

It's typical of my luck that I was in late the day that Nicki and Co. decided I was going to be the one to select the 20 worst-ever jokes. They'd all ganged up on me, y'see—"Good ole Greg can do it," they said, "He's got a great sense of humour." Well, y'know me, I've always been a sucker for flattery.

So I had to sort thru' sackloads of readers' letters and, when word got round, strangers kept trapping me in the lifts and refusing to let me out until they'd told me the worst joke they knew.

By the time I'd decided on the final line-up I was wishin' I'd never been talked into it!

Anyway, here goes with Greg's Groans . . .

1 *Where do tadpoles go to change into frogs?* The croak-room.

2 *On which side of the head is it best to wear a hat?* The outside.

3 *Little boy:* "Mummy, is it far to America?" *Mother:* "Shut up an' keep swimming."

4 *What's the definition of a mermaid?* A deep she-fish.

5 *Man in restaurant:* "Waiter, there's a fly in my soup."
Waiter: "Count yourself lucky sir, all the other customers have only got peas in theirs."

6 *A really scruffy, smelly old tramp goes into a pub with a pig under his arm. The man behind the bar says, "Where on earth did you get that?", and the pig replies, "I won it in a raffle."*

7 Why did the chicken cross the road? When it's ajar. (*This was one of Steve's—I always thought he had a weird sense of humour!*)

8 *Who created spaghetti?* Someone using his noodle.

9 *Pet-shop owner:* "Can I help you?" *Customer:* "Do you have any dogs going cheap?"
Pet-shop owner: "Sorry, sir, all our dogs go 'Bow Wow'".

10 *How d'you find out the weight of a whale?* Take him to the nearest whale-weigh station.

11 *Holidaymaker:* "Does water always come through the roof like this?"
Landlady: "Only when it rains."

12 *First man:* "Why's your dog wearing brown leather boots?"
Second man: "His black ones are at the menders."

13 A man is lying in the cinema stalls across three seats, so the usherette says, "If you don't move I'll report you to the manager". But the man just groans. The usherette says, "Alright then, what's your name?" The man groans again but manages to tell her. "And where do you come from?", she asks, and the man groans "The balcony".

14 *What does the ocean say when it sees the coast?* Nothing, it just waves.

15 An elephant goes into a pub and asks for a pint of beer. "That's seventy pence, please," says the barman. After a slight pause the barman says, just to be chatty, "We don't get many elephants in here nowadays". "I'm not surprised," replies the elephant, "with beer at seventy pence a pint."

16 *What's the best thing to do before you get off a bus?* Get on it.

17 *First man:* "What kind of dog is that?" *Second man:* "It's a boxer." *First man:* "Well, it can't be a very good one, just look at its face!"

18 *What has twenty-two yellow legs and two wings?* A Chinese football team.

19 *Girl:* "You remind me of the sea." *Boy:* "What, you mean all wild an' restless an' romantic?" *Girl:* "No, you make me sick."

20 *What did the mouse do when he came home and found his house on fire?* He dived in, dragged his children out, and gave them mouse to mouse resuscitation.

Well, have you been sick yet? I was ill for a week after reading thru' that lot!

There's just one advantage. Whenever the others in the office try to persuade me to do something I don't want to do, I just leer at 'em an' threaten to tell 'em a few good jokes . . . I've never seen anyone move so fast!

WILD BOY LES NO MORE!

Early last year the mere mention of Leslie's name had Tam wringing his hands in despair! It seemed that Les was up to his eyes in trouble and always hitting the headlines. Rumours were flying all over the place and some of them were pretty nasty.

But the lad was innocent! An' now Les is so careful about staying on the right side of the law that he hardly strays outside his door.

Behind him are the days when he'd speed around in flash cars just for kicks. Or sneak out to parties in disguise and not come home until the early hours of the morning. That sort of life caused far too many headaches and Les hated the reputation he was getting as the wicked one.

We're glad for him—and we always knew it was only naughtiness in him—never anything worse!

NOT SO SWEATY, BETTY!

While everyone's sizzlin' an' sweatin' in the hot sun, we'll show you how to keep your super cool an' stay fresh!

Are you gettin' excited? Cos, it's time for your summer hols again! Whether you're goin' a-broad or just lazin' on a deck chair in your back garden, the effects of the sun'll be the same! So be prepared! Don't get caught out, then end up with sunstroke for the rest of your hols—cos you'll never meet any guys that way!

CHECK LIST!

If you're going away, here's a quickie check list to make sure you haven't forgotten anything—it'll be too late when you get there!

Cleansing cream; toner; flannel; soap; toothpaste an' brush; deodorant; suntan oil; body lotion; tanning lotion; tissues; cotton wool; make-up; towels; plasters; shampoo an' conditioner; t-shirts; jeans; shirts; dress; skirt; undies; bikini; shorts; hat; nightie; cardi; jumper; and last but not least sandals!

Don't take huge bottles of stuff with you. It'll only take up valuable space! Often you find little suitcases have small plastic bottles already inside them. They are ideal for things like your cleanser, and they're unbreakable too!

When you're packing, put all the clothes like trousers and skirts, that tend to crease easily, in first (an' wrap 'em in tissue paper if you have any.) Then they'll be undisturbed until you want 'em!

YOU'VE ARRIVED

Well you made it! Even tho' the first thing you did was to give all the Spanish in the airport a glimpse of your undies! You didn't do up your case properly did ya!

You arrive safely at your hotel, an' can't wait to get stripped off (an' put your bikini on, of course!). But be careful, cos it won't go smoothly!

YOU'RE LILY-WHITE!

Did ya ever stop to think when you were at home, that you might look a trifle pale when you got here? No? Well you will! Try bounding down to the beach lookin' like that! So play it crafty—give 'em the impression you've been here for weeks! Smooth on a fake tanning cream that also lets in the sun's rays. So you'll be getting brown, whilst you already look it!

Find a peaceful place, spread your towel down, and relax! Just let the sun do the rest.

THINGS THAT GO WRONG

What did we say about it not goin' smoothly? So you've stumbled among a few problems. Who

cares! They're easy to solve . . .

FRECKLEPUSS!

You're sitting lapping up the sun, but you seem to be developing oodles of freckles on your freckles! How d'you stop this? You're obviously a red head an' will have to watch out. Don't expose your face to the sun; wear a large brimmed sunhat—that'll shade it! You may find your skin is kinda sensitive too, so if you start lookin' like a lobster—you'll know what's cooking!

HAIRY MESS!

When you're gettin' ready to go to the local disco, you find your hair is lookin' like straw, cos it's so dry . . .

You can either go dressed as a scarecrow, or do something about it! Never leave your hair exposed in the sun for any length of time. Always wear a hat. Either one with a huge brim or a turban type'll do. Whenever you wash it, don't forget the ol' conditioner will you? Rub some in, an' comb it thru' an' leave it for a few minutes. When you rinse it, it'll be easy to comb an' feel very soft!

GUIDE!

FEELIN' SWEATY!

When you've been out in the heat for a while, you'll start to feel all tacky an' sticky.

Why not take a break! Pop back to the hotel an' have yourself a cool, cool shower!

Spray on some anti-perspirant deodorant, and you're all set to start again!

PEELIN' SHOULDERS

You've kinda over done it! An' now your shoulders are startin' to peel! You probably forgot your suntan cream first of all didn't you? Never go out in the sun without protectin' yourself! There are lots of different makes a-round so take a look for some-thing that's suitable for you. And keep renewing it whilst you're on the beach! But if you do let it happen, keep covered for a while. Rub some after-sun cream all over and keep your sun-top or t-shirt on. Cos when you start to sun-bathe, you have to take it easy. Just a couple of hours the first day, and gradually stay longer as the time goes on.

SHINE OUT!

Summer is a great time for wearing make-up, cos your skin is usually in good condition. The sun has dried out all your spots and left your complexion clear. Wear as little as possible, an' make it shiny! Smooth a moist-uriser all over your face, to combat any dryness, and then make your eyes shine.

EYES ALRIGHT!

Smooth a glossy eye shadow all over your eyes, 'specially under the brow bone! Finish with a couple of coats of mascara. Next how to make those lips extra kissable. Apply a coat of darker lipstick an' then make 'em really stand out by slickin' over lotsa gloss, like Max Factor Lip Potion.

WHAT TO WEAR

The easiest way to keep your super cool is to wear the right things. Stick to cotton, not man-made fibres like nylon or acetate. Wear just shorts an' a t-shirt during the day, then you can dress up in a long cool sexy dress for the exciting evening ahead of you!

45

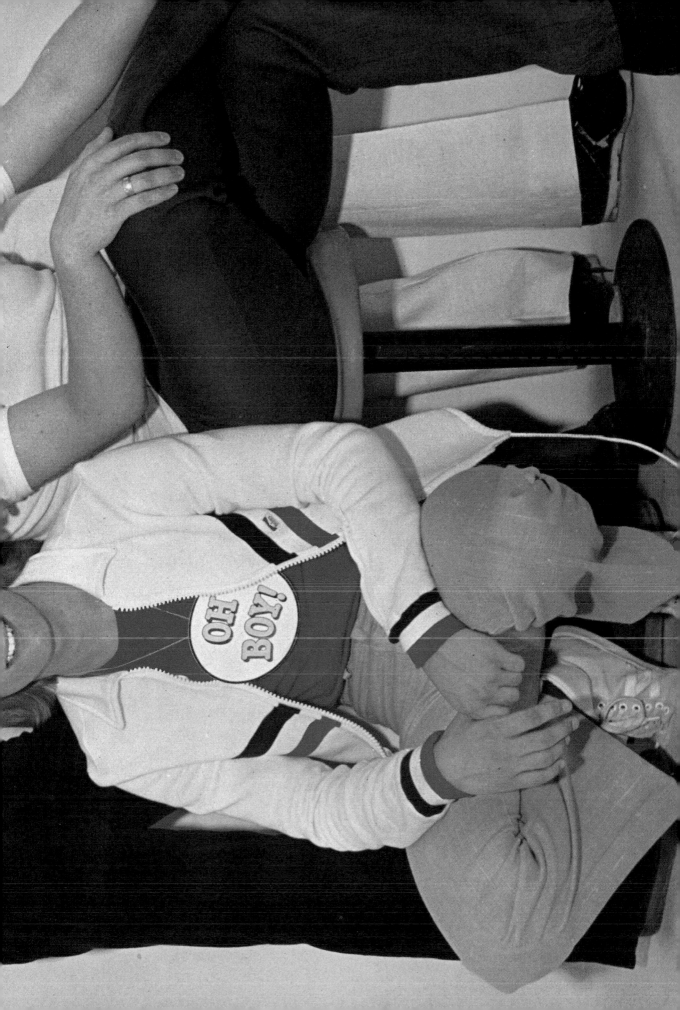

OH BOY'S SURVIVAL

BROWNED OFF? NO CHANCE!

Are you ready to face the whistling winds, dark nights, and blowin' leaves? Get prepared - cos autumn's back again!

GOT YOUR survival kit all packed an' ready? Cos you're gonna need it! No more loungin' on the grass sunning yourself—they don't say it's the season for 'bare trees an' chilly knees' for nothing!

Rub in lotsa pure olive oil to make your hair soft 'n' shiny!

It's kinda unpredictable weather, so be prepared! You could just be warm in a shirt one day, and it'll start snowin' the next! So keep nice 'n' cosy!

Hope you looked after your hair during the summer, or else the sun will have made it a right frizz by now! If it's out of condition, here's how to get it lookin' alright.

GOT THE FRIZZES!

So the sun's made it dry—okay? Well, what you need is to put moisture back in again! Next time you are gonna wash it, give yourself an extra half hour or so. Buy a large bottle of pure olive oil from your chemists. It's not expensive and will do the trick. Start by combing your hair thru' to get all the tangles out, and it brings the dirt nearer to the surface. Pour a little olive oil onto the palm of your hand, and rub it into your hair and scalp, gently. Comb thru' your hair, so the oil reaches the ends, and then wrap it up in a warm towel. Now you can leave it for about half-an-hour to soak in. After, give it a good wash using a mild Shampoo, like Silvikrin Almond Cream, giving it a good lather to get rid of all the oil. Condition well, so it's easy to comb thru' and blow dry it into a slick style. There—shining hair!

LANK 'N' GREASY

If, after all that sun, your hair's still on the greasy side, give it a few treatments with a special shampoo specially for oily hair, like Pears. This'll get it really clean without being too harsh. And don't forget to condition afterwards!

HAVE A CHANGE

Fancy a new style? It's a great way to keep that guy you met on your hols interested! He'll remember a tasty suntanned girl with shiny, well cut hair, so don't disappoint him! Your suntan might have faded by now, but there's no excuse for lettin' your hair get long 'n' straggly!

Have a good look around in magazines and books an' see if you fancy one of those styles. There are

Try a short swingy style that's neat 'n' tidy!

Add punch to long hair—layer the sides!

lots about, short 'n' long, so have a good think. How about a short 'bob' that has a gentle perm to keep it in shape. Or if you want long hair keep it trimmed regularly, and for a bit of interest, have the sides cut a little shorter than the back. It'll slope gently upwards, and will look very chic if when you go out, you put a few curlers in the end, so that it flicks back. Add a couple of cute hairslides, and wow!!

GO ON, NAIL 'EM

How are your nails? Not as good as they could be, or have you been biting 'em again!

With plenty of great nail polishes around, make it *this* autumn that you're gonna give up! Tell yourself "That's it! I aint havin' meaty stumps no more!" and when you feel like a nibble, grab your fella! When they start to grow, they'll be very weak, so give 'em a coating of Nailoid Plus with Nylon, to give 'em strength. Keep an emery board handy, an' every so often, file 'em.

Don't let your cuticles over-run rub a little cuticle cream into the nails to soften 'em up.

Soon, you'll be ready for some polish! Pick a shade to match what you're wearing. Or if you're clever enough paint one shade, leaving a shape like a moon, then fill in with another shade. Snazzy eh!

THINGS THAT GO WRONG

Running into a few problems?

Well hang around cos Liz has got the answers!

GHASTLY GOOSEBUMPS

You've discovered loads of little lumps on the tops of your arms that look like goosebumps, an' you're not even cold!

They're not really anything to do with the cold. It's a sign of bad circulation! So next time you have a bath or shower, give your arms a good scrub with a sponge to soften 'em up, and rub in lotsa body lotion.

PEELIN' SKIN

Your face's gettin' really dry an' is flakin' off on your cheeks.

Sounds like the dreaded lurgy, doesn't it?! T'isn't tho'! It's the wind—it really dries up the skin. Before you venture out in the morning, smooth in plenty of moisturiser like Nivea or Boots 17 Orange Blossom moisturiser.

ANNA LETS YOU INTO...

ABBA'S

When two great looking young couples spend their lives together, you can be sure there'll be love problems—rows, tantrums, secret hurried kisses in hotel corridors—if everyone doesn't watch it it'll be curtains for two beautiful friendships!

Anna of Abba knows all about the dangers, and she told us how the group stay together, and stay in love . . .

I SUPPOSE that everyone knows that we're two couples—Bjorn and I who're married and Frida and Benny who are engaged.

But what a lot of fans don't know is that there are two other couples in the band too!

Let me explain . . .

Firstly, there's the boys and the girls. Frida and I are often left alone when the boys go on business trips and we get very lonely.

We're both very bad at being by ourselves. After about five minutes I start brooding about all sorts of stupid things, which don't seem so silly to me in the mood I get into.

My baby, for instance—I used to worry a lot about him when he was left at home with a nanny. I'll always remember the day Bjorn and I got home from touring, and he didn't even recognise us!

I swore I'd never leave him for long again—but whenever I'm alone I worry about being away.

MOANING MINNIES

Frida's the same—she always misses Benny so much—she's a rather insecure person who needs a lot of love, perhaps because her mother died when she was very young . . .

But I'm making us sound like a couple of moaning minnies which we're not—honest! But we are a couple . . . we're very close, we sort out each other's problems, and she's like a real sister to me.

I'd never go behind her back, and I know she wouldn't deceive me. We trust each other completely.

The boys are the same.

They love to go off into the mountains near our holiday home together, leaving us behind to do all our chores!

And it's up in the snows that they often get the best idea for a song—even though they haven't even got a guitar to play it on. They have to keep the melodies in their heads and run back to the lodge to sing it to us!

GASPING

Once Benny ran all the way and was so out of breath he couldn't speak for about 20 minutes, let alone sing! He kept gasping something about SOS, and we thought Bjorn had fallen or something, but of course it was just an idea he'd had for a song—which we recorded later, as you may remember.

The boys are the business brains behind Abba and honestly without them I don't think we'd be where we are today.

They're always flying off to meetings—which keeps them good friends together, and means Frida and I stay close too.

There's another set of couples, too—me and Benny and Frida and Bjorn.

No, it's not what you're thinking—we often have chats together and I find Benny can help me when Bjorn's got one of his 'moods' on (which usually means he won't let me have my own way for a change!)

HOT PANTS

Like the time when Bjorn got all stubborn about me wearing a pair of gold hot pants cos he said they were too short!

I really fancied waltzing around the house in them, but Bjorn was quite firm about it.

So Benny got the idea he'd fiddle with our central heating, and he managed to force the heat up to almost tropical level.

Then he told Bjorn it was broken and we'd have to sit it out till the engineer arrived after the weekend. So we had no choice but to wander around in clothes that wouldn't be

LOVE SECRETS

too sweaty.

Within a few minutes Bjorn had his great hairy legs bulging out of some shorts, so did Benny and Frida was in a mini skirt.

But I just sat in a corner with a long dress on . . .

After a minute Bjorn gave in.

'OK, you win,' he smiled, as if he knew Benny and I had been up to our tricks—and I shot upstairs to get into them before he could change his mind !

MERCY

Frida and Bjorn often plot together, too—mostly to get me to do the washing up !

And that's how we work it. We're not really two couples, but six—so there can never be many real secrets between us.

And if there's any bad argu-ments we cool down the angry ones our own special way—we roll 'em in the snow until they scream for mercey !

It's a pity you don't have more snow in Britain—it sounds just the thing to quieten Greg down after he's told one of his strange jokes . . .

(Exit Greg miserably—he thought she'd found them de-lightful ! !)

ERIC— THE SADNESS HE HIDES...

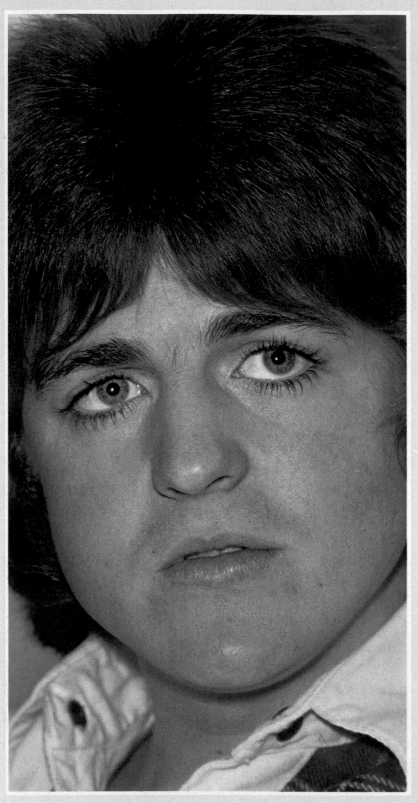

Although he's stuck by the Rollers, fame has never brought happiness to Eric. In his heart, he wishes he was still just an ordinary fella...

"IT'S music that matters to me. Not the applause and fans that being in a famous group brings, that all comes second.

"I know it's quite difficult to understand but all I've ever wanted is to be able to write songs that people would appreciate.

"Tam and I have had quite a few disagreements in the past because we never seemed to be able to record any of our own material but luckily that's all changed.

"Now the Rollers can pick the records we release ourselves, but even that hasn't fulfilled me really. I know it sounds kinda selfish but I'd much rather have respect for my music without having to put up with our life.

"You know, I don't mean to be moody and a bit irritable but sometimes it gets too much for me. I'm a loner at heart.

"When we're locked away in a hotel room somewhere the same memory always comes into my mind.

"It was years ago when Tam took Alan, Derek and I on holiday to Spain. We'd driven for hours and suddenly there was the sea in front of us, blue and shining under the sun.

"We didn't bother to get changed or anything, we just rushed for the water. And we threw ourselves in with yells that made everyone think we'd discovered gold or somethin'.

"That's how I feel, you see. When we're cramped up together because we can't walk in the street without getting mobbed, I feel just like I did in that hot dusty van.

"I want to jump up and escape from it all! But then I remember that there isn't really anywhere for me to go . . ."

BUGZY AND BERT

THE WORLD'S MOST LOVABLE RABBIT STRIKES AGAIN!

... Or would you rather be 'got'? Do our quiz and find out if you're the kind of girl that can keep a fella hanging on ...

DO YOU PLAY HARD TO GET?

1 He's been giving you the eye since you walked in—and you've been giving it back! Now it looks as if he's coming over. Would you—

(a) Head for the Ladies, but turn and give him a look before you go in?

(b) Say, "What kept ya, Big Boy?"?

(c) Turn your back on him and start filing your nails?

2 He chatted you up at the bus stop and arranged to meet you outside the cinema at eight the next night. Do you—

(a) Turn up with a couple of your friends and no money?

(b) Roll up just as he's starting to look at his watch and say, "We'd better hurry or we'll miss the commercials ..."?

(c) Grab a couple of back stalls and be waiting at 7.30?

3 You're up to your eyes in bubble bath when he phones and your mum shouts up the stairs, "It's Steve, can you come down?" Do you—

(a) Grab a towel and run down and drip into the phone?

(b) Shout, "No, I'll get my feet all dirty!" and hope he can hear?

(c) Tell her to say you'll ring him later?

4 He took you to the disco, bought you a meal and now you're getting into his car. "Where to now?" he says. Do you say—

(a) "Your place. My parents are in ..."?

(b) "My place please" and then, when you get there, say "Sorry I can't invite you in for coffee ..."?

(c) "If you drop me off at my place I might catch the midnight movie ..."?

5 You went to the party together but now he's over on the sofa chatting up this other bird. Do you—

(a) Chat to someone else and take no notice at all?

(b) Keep walking past the pair of them and saying, "Having a good time?"?

(c) Snuggle up between them on the sofa and say, "Bit of a squash with three on here, isn't it?"?

6 You're dancing with your friend when he sidles up and whispers, "Why don't you lose old Fatty and come over here with me ..." Do you—

(a) Say at the top of your voice, " 'Ere, Brenda, he called you an old Fatty ..."?

(b) Slink off to a dark corner and leave your mate dancing with a potted palm?

(c) Whisper "No thanks. She's a better dancer than you ..."?

7 Your friend comes up to the two of you and says, jokingly, "When are you getting engaged then?" Do you say—

(a) "Oh, just as soon as Robert Redford asks me ..."?

(b) "You've gotta be joking? He hasn't learnt how to tie his shoe laces yet ..."?

(c) "Oh, we couldn't get engaged! I haven't finished making the wedding dress ..."?

8 He's watching you from the other side of the room whilst one of his mates chats to you. In fact he's not chatting you up, just talking about his acne

problem. Do you—
(a) Giggle a lot and say, "Oog, Rodney, don't let Henry hear you say that!"?
(b) Get rid of him as soon as you can and go over and tell your fella what a jerk he was?
(c) Look absolutely fascinated and not even notice when your fella starts turning green?

9 He's with another girl but you can tell he fancies you. Finally he whispers, "Meet me tomorrow night down at the disco . . ." Do you—
(a) Clasp his hand, give him a wink, and say, "Can't wait . . ."?
(b) Look horrified and hiss back, "I couldn't possibly hurt Celia like that . . ."?
(c) Say, "Eh? Pardon? What *are* you muttering about?"?

10 If your steady boyfriend suddenly flung himself down on his knees and said "Darling, be mine forever (i.e. Will you marry me?)!" would you—
(a) Say, "But we hardly know each other..." even though you have been going out since you were six . . .?
(b) Shove a ring on his finger and say "Yeah, of course . . ."?
(c) Laugh in his face, and say "Get up off your knees before someone knights you .."?

YOUR SCORE:
1. a10 b0 c5; 2. a5 b10 c0; 3. a0 b5 c10; 4. a0 b10 c5; 5. a10 b5 c0; 6. a5 b0 c10; 7. a10 b5 c0; 8. a5 b0 c10; 9. a0 b10 c5; 10. a10 b0 c5.

WELL, HOW DID YOU DO?
0-30 Not so much hard to get as hard to *forget*! You're the kind of girl who doesn't believe in pulling her punches. You don't see any reason to pretend you're not interested when really you can't wait to get back and see his etchings! 'Course, some fellas like a girl with a bit of 'mystery' and aren't going to like your direct approach but we'd say most of 'em would love it!

35-65: Somewhere along the line you've got hold of the wrong end of the stick—you ain't just teasing these guys, you're torturing them! Whatever game it is you're playing—watch it! 'cos one of these days when you're rubbing the salt in he may just turn round and give you a taste of your own medicine!

70-100: Well, you've really got those fellas toeing the line and we bet they don't even know they're doing it! You just don't believe in giving all you've got in one go (or to one guy!) so these love-sick laddies just keep hanging around for more! It's fun, just so long as they keep trying but watch out for the day they stop—better get yourself 'got" before then!

GET PUZZLING WITH OUR

So you're thinking, who's this load of weirdos? Well, every one of them has a famous name!

Take a closer look at these faces and see if you can tell who they are. The clues are meant to make things a bit easier!

All the answers are on page 64.

1 Maybe he's putting a lot of emotion into singing the national anthem . . . or maybe it's just one of those too-tight tights!

2 A master of disguise—but his fingers give him away!

3 Not as you'd usually see him, but maybe in the running for a title?

4 Looks as though he doesn't like it much . . . but then he always was a bit of a rebel.

5 He may not have been much cop as William, but he's a lot nicer nowadays!

6 Here's a request—remember this face?

7 He's the brother of someone very famous. And that hat's a dead giveaway!

8 This lady's just one of a band of high-flyers.

9 Only five members in this fella's team—and they don't play Kricket on stage!

OH BOY TEASERS!

10 Presenting . . . in one of her more quirky roles . . .

11 Ahoy there! Come out from behind those dark glasses and identify yourselves!

12 A face of the future from the past—and his initials are the same as a sort of plastic sheet!

BRAIN BOGGLERS!

If your poor tired brains can stand it, here are three more puzzlers! The answers to all of 'em are on page 64.

THE NAME GAME!

Here's a list of names that everyone knows—but none of the stars here were born with 'em! So what are the real names of—
1. Gary Glitter; 2. Twiggy; 3. David Bowie; 4. Marc Bolan; 5. Alvin Stardust; 6. Cliff Richards; 7. Elton John; 8. Midge Ure; 9. David Soul; 10. Yan Style; 11. Paul Michael Glaser.

STAR-SPANGLED SENTENCES!

These sentences may not seem to make much sense, but hidden in each one is the name of a star. For example,
   It wont to and fRO Down and up again, hides the name ROD.
   Got it? Well, there're clues after each one to give you a bit of help!
1 Fancy a hat? Try this felt one! (*This fella's better known for his glasses than his hats!*)
2 I was laughing so much I was in hysterics. (*Rolling about with laughter, maybe?*)
3 Meat is cheap, but cheese is cheaper. (*This fella made his name using his feet!*)
4 She was as blind as a bat. (*This one's a lovely lady singer.*)
5 I held the candle over my head. (*He used to be a clown, but now we see him as he really is.*)

DETECT THE SUPERTEC!

If you can get the answers to the seventeen clues across in this puzzle, then you'll be able to read the name of the star in the centre column.

CLUES
1 Derek, lead singer of the group in clue 4.
2 Starsky's mate's real first name.
3 The monarch's favourite group?
4 See clues 1 and 11.
5 Brothers Chris and Eddie.
6 A group with twins, not as young as they sound!
7 Paul's surname, but it could be a Christian name too.
8 ..... Redburn of Kenny.
9 Roxy leader.
10 The dishiest deejay.
11 Mike, drummer of the group in clue 4.
12 Pat, successor to Ian.
13 The Longmuir that got away!
14 A manager who's nearly as well-known as his group.
15 Rob, Les, Pete and Kevin = ?
16 A county—or a singer.
17 This famous surname sounds the same as Woody's first name, but it's not spelt the same!

SINCE WE TWO PARTED

"Have a dance, Val?"

I shook my head mutley, but managed a smile at Geoff.

"Come on, don't be a drag," he persisted.

I bit my lip. "Honest, Geoff. I just don't fancy it at the moment." I stared past Geoff's head through the darkness of the disco to where I knew Tom was sitting, but it was no good, I couldn't see him.

Geoff shrugged. "I don't know what's wrong with you girls he said, "you should be falling over yourselves to get a dance with me."

I laughed, despite feeling like crying. "Perhaps later" I said, although the way I felt right then —well, it seemed I'd never feel like dancing again.

Geoff went away and I looked at his retreating back disinterestedly. I knew he liked me, even when I still had Tom he'd made that obvious, and he was nice enough—good-looking, too—but it was Tom that I loved, Tom who I'd always love. And Tom who had told me last week that I no longer had a place in his life.

A part of me still couldn't believe it—all he'd said to me, all we had been to each other, all gone to nothing.

I'd started going out with him early in the Spring. Not exactly love at first sight but pretty near it. Mutual attraction growing into something bigger, something special. It was the first summer that I'd had someone all of my own to share the days with. We'd swum, had picnics, gone for walks, and the sun shone all the brighter because Tom was there to share things. And now, those days had all gone, as if they'd never been. The tears began to well up again and I had to force them back. It would never do to cry here in front of everyone, to let everyone see how he'd broken my heart.

"Val" Lyn was tugging at my arm. "For goodness sake, cheer up. You look like the world's about to fall in on you or something."

"It already has".

"Look, how many nights are you going to be like this?"

"How can I tell?"

"Well, when you find out tell me and I'll come out with you when you're over it all. It's no fun going around with you like a wet doormat."

"You'd be like a wet doormat too" I said bitterly. "You've never been in love and been packed up."

"No, No, I haven't" she said. "But honestly, if I had I don't think I'd let myself get so downright miserable and pathetic about it. Surely it's better to appear as if you couldn't care less."

"Better? Better for who?"

"Well, it might make him realise what he's missing."

"And it also might make him think that I don't care about him, when I do care, very much And I want him to know it."

SIGHED

Lyn sighed. "I think you're mad. That nice Geoff Wallis keeps asking you to dance—I'd dance with him like a shot."

"Go right ahead."

"He doesn't want me—he wants you."

"And I only want Tom" I said stubbornly.

Lyn sighed again and got up to get us another coke each, leaving me to think about love and how unfair it all was.

I strained my eyes in the darkness but still couldn't see Tom, yet Lyn had said he was down here. He'd told me—promised me— that he wasn't giving me up for another girl, but I could no longer believe what he said. After all, he'd said that he would always love me, and what were those words worth now?

"It's not that I don't think a lot of you" he'd said on that awful night—the last time I'd seen him—"but I just want my freedom."

"But why?" I'd been bewildered, frightened, unable to keep back the tears.

"I don't know". He'd run his hands through his hair, looking embarrassed. "Things just change."

"I don't change" I'd cried desperately. "I still love you."

"Val, don't. Don't make it hard."

"Why should I make it easy!" I'd sobbed, crying in earnest now.

He looked upset himself, as if he couldn't cope with the situation, then he'd patted me on the shoulder, murmured something about "You'll be all right" and was gone.

I'd stood at my gate, staring after him, willing him to turn, praying that he'd come back— but he didn't, he didn't even wave. As he turned the corner it started to snow, very tiny sharp particles that stung my wet cheeks, but still I stood there until I felt frozen, turned into an icicle from my heart outwards.

"Hey, Val—how about that dance now?" I was jogged out of my dreams again by Geoff.

"I'll say this—you're persistent!"

"I've got to be with you. Come on!"

He took my hand and suddenly I thought—what the heck! I can dance with Geoff or not dance with Geoff just as the mood takes me. If I can't have Tom back what does it matter either way.

"OK" I got up just as Lyn was coming back with our drinks.

"My God!" she said. "It's actually moving!"

Geoff laughed and I pulled a face at her. I felt like telling her that the only reason I was dancing with Geoff was so that I could have a good look round and see who Tom was with, but I didn't want to hurt Geoff's feelings. As I said, he was nice enough.

We moved round as best we could on the crowded floor, my

chin resting on Geoff's shoulder and my eyes searching for Tom.

Suddenly I could see him! I shivered and jerked upright.

"What's up?"

"I . . . well, it's him."

"Tom?"

"Yes." It was a relief to be able to speak about him. To know that Geoff knew.

"He's with someone" I whispered into Geoff's shoulder.

"A girl you mean."

"Yes." It wasn't fair to burden Geoff with my problems, but he was there and I needed someone.

"I must see" I said.

Geoff loosened his hold and looked hard at me. "Are you sure?"

I nodded and stayed there, pretending to dance and looking all the time at Tom, my Tom, with someone else.

The girl was tall, almost as tall as him, with long dark hair. She was very pretty. She stood in front of Tom, laughing up at him, her long hair falling over her face. Tom was holding both her hands in his and looking at her as if he loved her—the way he used to look at me.

I stared and stared until it seemed that they would feel my eyes on them, until Geoff pulled me away.

"Come on" he said, "let's get some air."

We squeezed past everyone, across the dance floor and up the stone steps to where the disco met the street. Geoff flopped down beside me on the top step and we were quiet for a few moments, contemplating the empty street.

"I know how you feel" he said at last.

I shook my head. "I don't know how you can describe it" I said. "It's just sort-of-empty, as if it's not really happening."

TWO-TIMING

"Loving someone who doesn't love you" he said. His voice had changed and he was looking at me.

I didn't look up. Life was complicated enough. "Tell me about Tom" I said falteringly. "Has he been going out with her for long?"

"Truth?"

I shut my eyes. "Truth" I said.

"I saw him down here with her three weeks ago."

I sighed deeply. It was almost a relief to know the worst. "That's it then". Geoff squeezed my hand reassuringly but stayed silent.

"He was two-timing me."

"Now you know" Geoff said.

"It's better once you know. You can stop waiting and hoping and get back to the business of living." He put a comforting arm around me.

"The business of living doesn't interest me much."

"It will."

I stared up at the stars, wondering how long it would all take.

"Thanks for being around, Geoff."

"That's me all over—always available in times of need."

"I don't . . ." I hesitated, stuck for words. "I don't want you to think that I'm just using you because I haven't got Tom."

"I know what you mean—and anyway, I wouldn't mind if you were just using me."

"Why?" I looked away from the stars and looked at him.

"Because."

"Because what?"

"Because one day you're going to wake up and find that it's me in your mind instead of Tom".

I stared at him. It was too soon, much to soon to tell. It wouldn't be today, tomorrow or even next week, but in the end . . . well, it was a comforting thought.

It gave me something to hang on to . . . a promise of a new beginning.

EYES ALL POPPED AND BRAIN BOGGLED?

Well here're the answers from page 60!

POP EYE:
1 Freddie Mercury (Queen)
2 Ringo
3 Duke of Showaddywaddy
4 Steve Harley
5 Dennis Waterman
6 Tim Matheson from *The Quest*
7 Ron McKeown, brother of Les
8 Linda McCartney
9 Andy Walton (Kenny)
10 Pauline Quirke
11 Sailor
12 Peter Vaughan Clarke

THE STAR-SPANGLED SENTENCES GAME:

1 Fancy a hat? Try this fELT ONe! (ELTON)
2 I was laughing so much I was in hystERICs. (ERIC)
3 Meat is cheap, BUT CHeese is cheaper. (BUTCH)
4 She was bLIND As a bat. (LINDA)
5 I held the candLE Over my head. (LEO)

THE NAME GAME:—

1 Paul Gadd
2 Lesley Hornby
3 David Jones
4 Marc Feld
5 Bernard Jewry
6 Harry Webb
7 Reg Dwight
8 Jimmy Ure
9 David Solberg
10 Ian Style
11 Paul Manfred Glaser

DETECTED THE TEC?

Well, if you got Paul Michael Glaser you sure did!

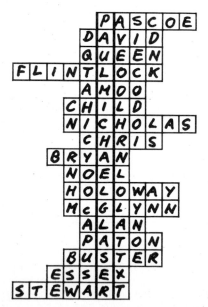

PASCOE
DAVID
QUEEN
FLINTLOCK
AMOO
CHILD
NICHOLAS
CHRIS
BRYAN
NOEL
HOLOWAY
McGLYNN
ALAN
PATON
BUSTER
ESSEX
STEWART

NICKI'S

Phew! Two whole pages just for li'l' ol' me! ('Cept for the rotten answers!) 'Course I always knew I'd be a star—people like me just can't help being loved, adored, admired . . . So come on, somebody, *prove* it will ya!

But meanwhile . . . get stuck into this lot!

SHOCK SECRET No I!

SHAME ON YER, ROD!

For a fella who likes flashing around in tight white trousers with a lot of sexy ladies, Rod Stewart's got awful shy all of a sudden!

Cos when he was in America his Romeo reputation got around to a coupla those glossy girlie mags and they asked Rod–ever so nicely!–if he'd mind shedding the tartan for a bit and posing for a centrefold!

Oooh, was he shocked!

Didn't know where to put himself! Even the offer of 8,000 dollars couldn't tempt him!

"It all seemed rather cheap," he says. But actually, we reckon he just didn't want 'em to see his Marks & Sparks undies!

OOOH, YOU ARE AWFUL!

Ever wondered what your kid brother gets up to in the bathroom? Liza Stewart of Rotherham knows and now she wishes she didn't . . .

ALL WASHED UP!

I'd started running my bath and run back into my room to get all the gear—trannie, waterproofed book, eyebrow tweezers etc.—when I suddenly heard the door slam and realised my little brother (the worst thing since deep-freeze knickers) had dived in there!

I stood there fuming but about ten minutes later he came out lookin' all innocent and sayin' he'd just been brushing his teeth (they were still green).

Quickly I ran in and checked.

No nails in the soap. Nothing unpleasant on my flannel. Toothpaste hadn't been swapped for hair-removing cream. Funny . . . everything looked okay!

It wasn't until I'd thrown off my clothes and jumped into the bath that I realised the little angel had done it again.

There was a sort of nasty squelching noise and this sludgy thing shot down towards the plug—Eric, my darling brother's plastic toad!

Got my own back tho', didn't I?

Next time he took a bath, I made him wash!!

GREATEST HITS!

SHOCK SECRET No 2!

HARLEY'S HORRORS!
Steve Harley's a mighty strange fella y'know. Some people might say downright odd. But not me!

And if you've ever wondered where he gets some of those eerie songs of his from, I can tell ya!

Nope, I haven't been peering through his bathroom key-hole to see if he sings in the bath—I don't need to. Cos Steve gets all his inspiration whilst he's asleep!

S'true—honest! Apparently there's not a night passes when our hero isn't tossing and turning under the ol' fluffy pink blanket!

He has a nightmare every night and each morning he wakes up with a new song!
Neat, eh?

GOOD GAME?
Urrrrgh! Bruce Forsyth–he makes me wanna scream! I s'pose he thinks it's funny being nasty to people but if he stood there laughing at me whilst I got tangled up with some pottery or something, I'd soon wipe the smile off his face!

I'd tie his skinny little legs in knots and give him some free dental treatment—with my boot! —that's what I'd do!

Ooooh, I feel better for that!
Nicola Green, Littlehampton.

SWITCH OFF!
My own vote for Instant Turn-Off Of The Year goes to . . . Nicholas Parsons! He wins my Creepo Prize—a full length mirror, so's he can make *himself* sick!.

DUFF DANCERS!
They're a bunch of over-sized poodles who 'dance' in a lot of silly dresses that the Ugly Sisters wouldn't be seen dead in, smiling into the camera with their toothy grins and waving their arms and legs around like Magnus Pyke on a bad day! Yep, that's right! They're Legs & Co!

I wouldn't watch 'em but my dad won't let me switch off!
Alison Fielding, Walthamstow.

FANCY THEM!

Couldn't make up my mind, could I? Didn't know which tasty fella to pick—well, it's tough with all these good-lookers around! So I've picked my three fave-raves—cos they've all got something a little bit different!

SOMETHING COOL...
Can't get much cooler than Bryan Ferry can ya? He's so smooth his clothes slip off! Only trouble is, he's got a lady to match . . . So how's about it Jerry, eh? Fancy this one-way ticket to Outer Mongolia . . .?

SOMETHING HOT...
Yep, when Rod's on stage even his scarf sweats! An' that's *before* he starts moving! Ooooh, once those hips start swaying, there's no holding me! Quick somebody, bring me a glass of water—not to *drink* you fool !— to throw over meself !

AN' SOMETHING TOUGH!
When all the girls see him they just go 'ape'! An' no wonder, cos King Kong's just about the biggest, cuddliest fella you could ever hope to come across. Well actually, I hope I *don't* come across him, but he's nice to look at, ain't he?

CRUEL TO BE KIND...

"She's either very unkind to them . . ."

WHO IS THIS — ER . . . PERSON, TINA?

TED, MUM — WE MET LAST WEEK AT FREDA'S HOUSE. WE'RE ALL THINKING OF GOING ON HOLIDAY TOGETHER IN THE SUMMER.

WELL, I SUGGEST HE HAS A BATH BEFORE HE COMES HERE AGAIN!

MUM — !

HUH?

MUM, YOU SHOULDN'T SPEAK TO MY FRIENDS LIKE THAT!

THEN GET HIM OUT OF THE HOUSE AND I WON'T HAVE TO!

"So exit Ted . . ."

TED — I'M SORRY . . .

YEAH, WELL YOUR MUM'S A RIGHT MOUTHY BIRD AIN'T SHE! YOU'RE WELCOME TO 'ER!

"After a week . . ."

WHERE'S THAT FRIEND OF YOURS? TED, WASN'T IT? HE'S NOT BEEN ROUND FOR YOU LATELY.

YOU NEEDN'T WORRY, HE WON'T BE BACK, MUM.

"Her other method was even worse . . ."

I THOUGHT YOU SAID YOUR MA WAS HOME, TINA.

SHE IS. UPSTAIRS — AND WITH LUCK SHE'LL **STAY** THERE!

68

"We went out weekends, too . . ."

WATCH IT, REF . . . OR I'LL SET MY GIRL ON YOU!

YEAH! I'LL COME DOWN THERE AND SORT YOU OUT!

"Mum didn't know about Burt. Not even when . . ."

I LOVE YOU, TINA – I WANT TO MARRY YOU!

OH, DARLING, DO YOU? I LOVE YOU SO MUCH . . .

"He took me to see his folks . . ."

D'YOU KNOW, YOU'RE THE FIRST GIRL OUR BURT'S EVER BROUGHT HOME. HE MUST **LIKE** YOU, DEAR.

I HOPE SO, MRS. CONWAY.

BURT SAYS HE WANTS TO MARRY THAT GIRL, MOTHER.

WELL, HE COULD DO WORSE. SHE SEEMS A NICE LITTLE THING TO ME . . .

"Eventually, the moment I'd put off for so long . . ."

YOU SEEM A BIT UP-TIGHT – WHAT'S WRONG, LOVE?

OH – ER . . . NOTHING. MY MUM'LL BE DOWN IN A MOMENT . . .

OHH, I DIDN'T KNOW YOU HAD COMPANY, TINA.

I **TOLD** YOU I WAS BRINGING BURT HOME, MUM.

GOOD EVENING, MRS. REYNOLDS.

"I could see what role she was going to adopt with Burt. The sweep 'em off their feet routine . . ."

71

SAY HELLO TO LOVE EVERY WEEK IN OH BOY!

1 Keith Markham, 18 from Brighton, is a water-skiing instructor. Funny how a lot of girls are taking up water-skiing nowadays . . .

2 You all know who this is . . . but who's that dishy fella in the background? He looks just like Les McKeown . . .

3 Two for the price of one in this pic of Tim and Keith Atack of Child. On their own they're enough for any girl, but together . . . two much!!

4 Gary Wolfe from Uxbridge works in an antique shop . . . the brass bed comes from an antique market . . . not bad for a coupla antiques, eh?

3 PIN-UPS!!

Here's a quick flash-back over some of the bodies bared before your eager eyes in Oh Boy . . .

5 Peter Van Day was another of the fellas brave enough to bare his chest . . . no mistaking this guy from the dolls!

6 Michael Phillips, in his job as a photographer's assistant, should be used to flashes. We're glad he gave us this one!

7 No, not the latest in summer fashion, but Paul Michael Glaser as the Great Houdini . . . anyone got a set of skeleton keys?

8 D'you remember this naughty peek at model Bob's vital statistics? How could you ever forget it!

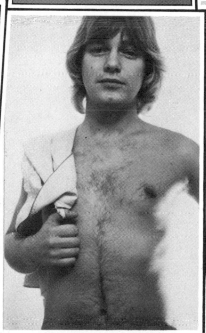

9 This is a sort of half-Moone, cos it's John, one half of the Moone Brothers. So how'd you like to be promised the Moone?

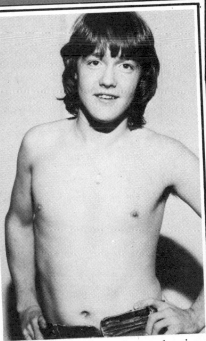

10 Last but not least in our luscious line-up is Keith Chegwin from Oh Boy's very own swop service. Any offers?

YOU NEED HELP?

Here are the six most common problems we have to deal with.

THE GIRL WHO'S UNSURE...

Tim was the boy me and all my mates used to fancy like mad. He always had loads of girlfriends tho', and they were all real knockouts! So you can imagine my surprise when he actually asked *me* out!

It was great at first, you know, cloud nine and everything, but we've been together now for four months and well, the trouble is, I'm so scared of losing him that I'm ruining everything. I get jealous when he even looks at another girl and on the nights he doesn't see me I get so upset and miserable. What can I do?

Marie, Portsmouth.

Think yourself lucky you've got such a nice fella. Any other kind would've ditched you long ago! The first thing to do is stop being so concerned with what Tim might be about to do and get your tiny brain working on what you're gonna do yourself. Your fella has become your whole life and it just won't do! Get interested in things other than him, go out with your mates more and make plans that don't always include Tim.

Secondly let your poor old mum in on the act and tell her to give you a quick clip around the ear'ole when she sees you mopin' about the place!

Finally, have some confidence in yourself. You're obviously just as much of a knockout as those girls he used to date— as far as Tim's concerned. And that's what counts isn't it?

THE GIRL WHO'S CONFUSED...

I'm pretty fed up with fellas at the moment. Honestly, they all seem to be after one thing!

Take my last boyfriend, Paul, for instance. We got on really great and everything would've been fantastic except he would keep trying it on all the time. I kept telling him I didn't want to and everything but he just wouldn't listen and in the end I just had to stop seeing him. I know some of my mates go all the way with their boyfriends but I don't think I should just because they do. It's not that I don't feel attracted to boys in that way—it's just that I don't feel it'd be right for me at the moment. I'm all confused . . .

Sue, Ayr.

Oh dear—reckon you've had a bit of bad luck with the fellas you've been out with so far. They're not *all* like that tho'. Honest!

You obviously don't have any trouble getting boyfriends anyway and we reckon it's really just a matter of time before you meet someone who'll respect your feelings.

But in the meantime don't forget that fellas are human too and sometimes it's possible for girls to lead them on and get 'em all worked up without even realising. *You* wouldn't be doing that would you? Think about it cos it could be you're getting your wires crossed!

When all you want is a kiss 'n' cuddle he might think you're asking for something else . . .

THE GIRL WHO'S NEVER HAD A FELLA...

You probably won't believe this, but I've got to the ripe old age of sixteen and have never had a boyfriend! I'm really beginning to think there must be something desperately wrong with me. It's not that I'm ugly or anything but for some reason boys just don't ask me out.

Could you please tell me what I'm doing wrong cos I'm so worried about it.

I've just left school (it was a girls' school) and started work in an office. There're lots of girls there and quite a few of my age. They've all got boyfriends, it seems, and spend a lot of time talking about them.

I feel so left out and miserable.

Jenny, Ripon.

Well, we do believe you cos you're not the only one, see? Guess you haven't had much of a chance to meet many fellas yet.

The main thing is to try very hard to stop worrying so much. Make friends with the girls at work-it doesn't matter what you talk about—I'm sure they've got other interests as well as fellas!

Talk to your parents about it too cos when they realise how unhappy you are, I'm sure they'll want to help.

What you've gotta do is go out and meet lots of people and be friendly towards them ('specially fellas) but remember, when a boy sees a girl with DESPERATE stamped across her forehead he's likely to run ten miles . . .

And there's an answer to every one...

THE BOY WHO'S PAINFULLY SHY...

I'm writing to you cos although I'm a boy I'll try anything once! You see, it's really awful—I'm so shy I just don't know what to do. Honestly it's really that bad.

Being like this ruins everything. I stammer and blush at school if I'm asked anything in class or for the slightest reason. And as for girls, well, I cross the road rather than have to speak to a girl I know from school or somewhere.

My parents are always telling me to 'buck-up' and stop moping about the house but I get so miserable. Anyway I'd rather stay in than make a fool of myself.

Jamie, Hereford.

Glad you did write to 'Oh Boy' Jamie cos we like to hear from boys as well as girls, and the amount of letters we get from fellas with exactly the same problem is nobody's business!

First of all you must realise that shyness is usually caused by worrying about what other people think of you. Of course it's only natural to care about what other people think, but there are degrees you know!

So, the best thing to do is to think of something else. Try and forget about yourself and get interested in what you're doing or who you're talking to instead of worrying whether you've got toothpaste on the end of your nose or something even worse!

THE BOY WHO KEEPS GETTING CHUCKED...

I wonder if *you* can tell me what I'm doing wrong cos no-one else seems to be able to.

I'm a good-looking fella, I reckon. I like trendy clothes, dancing, playing electric guitars, cars and football. I've got a good job so I've got money.

I never have any trouble getting girl-friends (I've had plenty in my time). My problem is I can't seem to keep 'em. I'm pretty sure I haven't got bad breath or B.O. or anything so I can't understand why it is that every girl I've been out with has finished with me after about two weeks. It's not as though they aren't keen to begin with-honestly I have to fight them off at times!

Noel, Reading.

You mean you really don't know? Bet any of those girls would've told you in no uncertain terms if only you'd asked!

It seems as if you don't really give the impression that girls mean much to you at all.

Of course it'd be stupid to think you shouldn't have interests but if you really want a steady girlfriend as well, you're gonna have to show a bit of interest in *her* direction too.

Also it looks as if you could be placing a bit too much importance on money and all it can buy. Sure, we're all crazy about it but we've gotta realise MONEY ISN'T EVERYTHING. That corny saying about the best things in life being free rings true sometimes, doesn't it?

THE BOY WHO WON'T BE CHANGED...

My girlfriend Sara's driving me round the twist! Everything was great to start with but now I just can't seem to do anything right as far as she's concerned.

She used to like me for what I am but now she's just doing her best to make me into a different person. Honestly, if it isn't my hairstyle she's on about it's the colour of my shoes or my job.

She keeps pointing out blokes she thinks look good and tries to get me to buy the same sort of clothes they wear.

It really gets on my nerves cos I want to be **me** not a replica of someone else.

D'you think there's any chance of changing **her**?

Tim, Llandudno.

'Fraid not, Tim. Sounds like Sara's decided on the kinda guy she wants and is determined it's gonna be you whether you like it or not. She's a born nagger and *nothing's* gonna change her, so don't waste your energy trying.

Better tell her this leopard ain't gonna change his spots for her or anyone else and if she doesn't like it she knows what to do about it ...

Have YOU got a problem? Write in to us and we'll do our best!
Greg and Jenny, Oh Boy, King's Reach Tower, Stamford St., London SE1 9LS.

THE BOY ON THE 6.15

Jilly was in love.
Oh, she knew it was stupid all right. Well, maybe not exactly stupid, but just the sort of thing other people wouldn't understand. She knew what they'd say. You *can't* be in love with somebody you don't even know.

But she was.

She saw the boy every day on her way home from work on the 6.15 commuter special. He had dark hair and nice brown eyes and the sort of smile that made you think of the sun suddenly appearing from behind a cloud.

The very first time Jilly spotted him she got that strange feeling in her heart, and knew that all the stories she'd heard about love at first sight could sometimes be true. True for *her* anyway, if not for the boy.

Every evening sitting on the train Jilly would watch him, and let her mind wander off into hazy, pleasant dreams. Imagining she was his girl, planning out the sort of dates they would have together. Silly things like that. Knowing in her heart it would never be anything more than a dream.

The boy on the 6.15 never noticed her, of course. Well, he wouldn't. He was too wrapped up in the other girl who was with him on the train every evening. Slim, blonde and pretty, the sort of girl who made Jilly feel like Cinderella *before* she found her fairy godmother.

They always got off at the same station as Jilly, at the end of the line, and one night going along the platform she heard the blonde girl say, "Hurry up, Mike, I don't want to miss my bus," and the boy had replied, "OK, Susan, don't panic."

Mike. So that was his name. It made Jilly feel happy to know that. As if it somehow brought him closer to her, made him seem more real.

She wasn't so happy about having learned the blonde girl's name at the same time. That was something she could have done without, thanks very much. She didn't want the blonde girl to grow any more real than she already was.

After all, it was bad enough having to watch Mike and Susan —since that seemed to be her name—sitting together on the train every evening, talking in soft whispers, exchanging little looks and smiles, lost in their own private world. Not noticing anything or anybody else.

They were in love, Jilly thought. It stood out a mile. As plain as the nose on a monkey's face was what her mother would have said, whatever that meant.

And every evening when she got off the train Jilly would go home with a deep ache in her heart, wondering why she had to be in love with a boy who didn't even know she existed, a boy who already had a girl he was crazy about.

SADNESS

Sometimes life just didn't seem fair.

Then one Monday night Jilly got in the train and saw Mike sitting further along the carriage. Alone.

A wild rush of hope swept through Jilly, and she had to struggle to make herself think sensibly.

Maybe Susan was just on holiday. Or sick. Or anything. Just because she wasn't there it didn't *have* to mean she and Mike had split up . . .

But all the same Jilly thought she could see a sadness in Mike's face. And she wondered what had caused it.

Every night that week she managed to get into the same carriage as Mike, half-expecting every time that Susan would appear again. But she didn't. And the sadness didn't leave Mike's face either.

On the Friday night Jilly found herself sitting directly opposite Mike on the train. For a long time she sat there thinking, hardly breathing, wondering how she could start a conversation with him.

Then she realised Mike was looking at her with a slightly curious, puzzled expression.

"Is anything wrong?" he asked.

"Wrong?" Jilly had to fight to stop herself from stammering. It had happened at last. Mike had actually *spoken* to her. "What d'you mean?" she asked, as calmly as she could.

"I just wondered. The way you were sort of staring at me. Like I'd a spot on my nose or something."

"Was I? I'm sorry, I didn't mean . . ." Jilly could feel herself starting to go red.

"That's OKay," Mike said, smiling. "Nobody minds a pretty girl staring at them. Sort of flattering really."

Jilly thought for a minute, wondering what to say next.

"Your . . . er . . . your friend isn't with you tonight," she ventured finally. "I hope she isn't sick or anything."

"My friend? Oh, you mean Susan." Mike frowned. "No, she isn't with me. And I don't suppose she will be, ever again."

Something about the way he said it made Jilly look up quickly, hope springing in her heart. But Mike was looking puzzled again.

"Hey, I don't get it. How did you know I'm usually with Susan? I mean . . ."

"Oh, I'm on this train every night too," Jilly laughed, feeling really happy all of a sudden, and wanting to laugh about everything. "You get to recognise some of the

passengers, don't you?"

"Oh." He looked surprised. "I've never noticed you."

That hurt a little. But she reminded herself that while he was with Susan he couldn't be *expected* to notice other girls.

Only Susan was gone now. Forever, it seemed.

They chatted to each other for the rest of the journey. Jilly told him about her work, and Mike told her something about himself and Susan. They worked in the same office block in town, he said. That was how they'd first met and fallen in love.

When the train reached their station they were still talking, and Mike asked Jilly if she'd like to have a coffee somewhere.

"Guess I've got a cheek asking you," he said. "No reason why you should sit and listen to all my troubles, but . . ."

"I'd like to."

Cheap plastic ducks decorated the walls of the coffee bar they went to, but to Jilly they looked beautiful. Everything did. She felt as if every dream in the world was coming true.

But first she had to find out about Susan.

"What happened?" she asked Mike. "You said on the train that she wouldn't be with you ever again. Does that mean it's all over?"

"Yes. For good."

"Why? I mean, if you really loved each other . . ."

"She thought we were getting too serious. Something like that anyway. So we'd a big fight." He gave an awkward shrug. "She's started taking the bus all the way home from work now. It's half an hour longer, but she thinks it's better that way. Instead of travelling with me, she means."

"Do you still love her?" Jilly asked quietly.

"I guess so. It isn't something you can switch off just like that."

Jilly felt sad for him. She wanted to put her hand over his and tell him he'd forget Susan soon, that there were other girls in the world.

LAUGHED

Meaning one girl in particular, of course.

"Funny you noticing us on the train like that, " he said.

"Yeah, isn't it?"

"But it's even funnier that I never noticed *you* before. Can't think how I missed you. I must've been blind."

"Well, maybe that blonde hair of Susan's was blocking the view."

"Yeah, maybe. It's bad for the eyesight is that. "Mike laughed. "But not any more."

Jilly felt her cheeks glowing with happiness. That feeling didn't go away, even when Mike said he'd have to go. Just for a moment she half-wondered if he would kiss her . . . but it was too soon for anything like that.

"See you Monday night on the train." Mike smiled. "I'll keep an eye open for you."

Jilly ran all the way home, and when her mother asked what she was looking so pleased about she just laughed happily.

"Oh, it's nothing. I just like riding on trains, that's all."

All weekend she looked forward to the Monday. Thinking of seeing Mike again, and what they would say to each other this time. Thinking how wonderful it would be.

On the Monday night when she left the office she was walking on air. She rushed into the railway station and climbed aboard the 6.15.

After a moment she spotted Mike sitting further along the carriage, and started towards him. Then she stopped dead in her tracks.

Mike wasn't alone. Beside him was a flash of familiar bright blonde hair, and he and Susan seemed lost in conversation, lost in each other.

Mike looked up and spotted Jilly. He smiled and waved to her and she tried to smile back to show she was pleased for him. But he didn't notice. His head had already turned towards Susan again, to listen to something she said.

They were in love, Jilly thought. Stood out a mile for everybody to see. And she didn't even want to wonder why or what had happened over the weekend to bring them together again. Once more they were lost in a world of their own, and there was no room in it for anybody else.

Jilly sat in a window seat, and felt the tears slowly start to come to her eyes. Silly to feel as if the greatest romance of her life had just finished, she thought. Something couldn't finish when it had never really started in the first place, could it?

But the tears were running down her cheeks, and in her heart dreams were slowly crumbling, like petals falling from a dying flower.

I MADE HIM STEAL FOR ME!

Name Linda Nichols
Age 16 **Birthplace** London
Linda took Paul for the biggest ride of his life...

IF I'M HONEST it was the car that first attracted me to Paul. I mean, I'm not an expert on cars, but it looked a really classy one. Anyway it was sleek and expensive-looking—the complete opposite of the broken down jalopies boys used to take me out in.

And Paul always looked smart. Even in jeans, he looked like the kinda person who has pots of money.

I often saw him around, and I knew people who knew him, so I used to say hello, and we'd smile at one another. I used to think about him a lot. But I'm not sure if I really fancied him. Y'see he was pretty good looking, but not that special.

Well, one evening I met him at a party, and got chatting to him. He seemed fairly keen and when the party started to wind up he offered to drive me home. Wow!

It was amazing to find myself sitting in that car at last, after all the times I'd dreamt about it. It was like riding on air—sheer luxury! Halfway home we stopped for a bit of snogging, and Paul told me how he'd always fancied me, and how he wanted to go out with me a lot more. Then we were speeding along again.

When he dropped me off, Paul said, "Hope you enjoyed the ride" with a sorta glint in his eye that showed he really meant the halfway stop. And I said, "Yes, it was fantastic!" But I really did mean the drive!

Paul was over the moon about me and I was nuts about his car. I reckoned we'd get along fine.

Next night Paul took me out. "Where shall we go?" he asked so I said, "Wouldn't mind having something to eat, I haven't had a thing all day." "Where?" he said screwing his face up as though he was trying to think of the best place. So I named the best restaurant in the area. I mean it was the sort of place I'd only dreamed of going to when I'd been dreaming about Dad winning the pools.

"Okay," said Paul, and off we went. Well, it really was good. I mean I was treated like a queen by the waiters, and I must admit I felt like a film star!

After that we saw quite a bit of each other. And every time I got Paul to take me somewhere nice. He never seemed to mind paying.

Then there were the presents. I found I only had to look in a shop window at something and keep on and on about how much I liked it and Paul would buy it for me. He bought me a ring and a necklace that must have set him back quite a bit.

All this time Paul seemed to be liking me more and more. But I never really thought about him and what he meant to me—apart from him buying meals and things.

Then one day we had a terrible row, the first one we'd ever had. Paul said we ought to just stay in sometimes instead of always going out for expensive meals and so on.

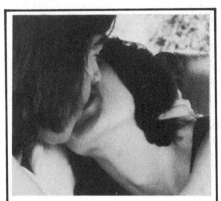
Halfway home we stopped for a bit of snogging . . .

Well, I got really angry and called him a Scrooge and a meanie. And he just stormed off and left me.

It was all right next day, tho', cos he turned up with a lovely bracelet for me, and took me out.

But a few days later I began to get worried. Paul didn't come round or phone for a couple of days. I thought maybe he'd had second thoughts after our row. Then the time turned into a couple of weeks and still no word from him.

I could've jumped for joy when Mum yelled out that Paul's car was outside the house.

I dashed out and was going to fling my arms round him. Only it wasn't Paul who got out of the car, it was a complete stranger . . .

"What are you doing with Paul's car?" I said, a bit stunned.

"It's not Paul's car—it's mine," he said. "I'm Geoff, Paul's older brother. I lent him my car while I was working abroad."

"Well, where's Paul?" I said "I haven't seen him for ages."

"Paul's been in trouble," he said, "Y'see he stole a lot of money from the place where he works."

"But why should he steal, he's got loads o' money?"

"You're joking," said Geoff, "Paul's just a clerk. He earns hardly anything. He even borrows most of his clothes from me. Y'see he used up all his savings on you, and stole when you wanted more. You sucked him dry. Luckily I came back in time to pay for what he stole, so the police won't be involved. And I've made Paul realise what type of girl you are, only interested in money. I've found him a job up North, so you won't be getting your claws into him again. I just promised him I'd come and tell you. And I wanted to have a look at you. If it's any consolation you don't look the type you are." And then he got in the car and just drove off.

I still feel awful about it—I can't wear any of the stuff Paul gave me. I mean I should have known. Paul never spent much on himself when we went out, he'd never have much to eat while I was gorging myself. He was obviously trying to save money.

And he must have thought a lot of me, cos he wasn't the type to steal. I hate that word "type", cos I don't like to think of myself as the money grabbing type. But I was. Well, I've learnt my lesson now. I'm thro' with flash restaurants and cars. I reckon I'll be lucky ever to find another guy who loves me as much as Paul did. But if I do—it won't matter if he's poor.

THE OH BOY CASEBOOK
18 AUG. 77

GREG—THIS IS YOUR LIFE!

Get your hankies out, folks! It's tear-jerker time! And you can guess who the jerk is, can't you? That's right—welcome to Greg's page . . .

Working with Steve can be a pretty sickening experience at times.

Y'see, Steve seems to attract the sort who like to write letters. Can't think why—s'pose they feel sorry for him, being all puny an' shrivelled like that. All I know is that it's having a terrible effect on him.

When he sees each day's delivery of letters on his desk, a sorta ugly grin cracks his face. Then he looks to see if I've got any mail which I haven't—so his grin gets wider. By the time he's got round to sittin' down an' counting 'em, his grin's so wide that it looks like the top of his head's come loose.

But I'm not going to be downhearted. Nope, I've convinced myself I'm better than Steve (one look at him and I was convinced). Y'see, I've told myself that all my fans form the great silent majority.

I mean, I'm pretty stunning to look at, I'm witty an' clever (and modest)—what more d'you want? So even though Steve gets all the ones who write letters, I reckon I've got millions of girls just waiting for the next word to flow from my pen and who're too busy just *thinkin'* about me to write letters.

I've got to think that really, or I'd never be able to face Steve again.

Here comes another delivery of mail now—you can always tell by the yelps of pleasure from Nicki and Liz as the post-boy pinches their bums.

This time, when Steve gets all the letters, I won't go green with envy (*Oh, go on Greg—it'd make a change from your usual sickly yellow—Nicki*). No, I'll just think of all my fans out there somewhere.

Who needs fan mail anyway? (*Shut up Greg! You're breaking our hearts!!—Nicki*)

THE SNEEZIN SEASON!

Time for freezin' knees, big red noses, an' nasty cracked lips! So get out your woollies, and have fun!

IT'S GONNA be perishin' so make sure you're ready for it! Don't go without your coat, then moan when ya start snifflin', cos it serves ya right! If you find things goin' wrong, never fear, Liz's here!

wash your hands, smooth in lotsa hand cream. When you go out, don't forget your gloves—they'll protect you from the cold. If you don't fancy wearing ordinary gloves, try a pair of scrooge gloves, then you can be mean with your money!

SORE 'N' PRICKLY!

You've been out in the wind, an' your eyes are all sore 'n' runnin'!

If they're feelin' sore an' prickly give 'em an eye bath, like Optrex, that'll sooth 'em! Or even cheaper, shut your eyes for 10 mins with a couple of cold tea bags resting on 'em!

RED CONK!

You've come home with a bigger, redder nose an' face than you've seen on Rudolf, an' nothin' seems to make it go!

You could always pretend you're

3.
Keep your lips soft 'n' kissable with a touch of lip salve!

1.
Grab yourself a pair of scrooge gloves an' be an ol' meany!

WHITE AS A GHOST!

Your face looks like you've had a bit of a scare!

Even if you got a suntan in the summer, it would've faded by now, so fake a bit of colour! Wear a darker foundation than your colour an' then add lotsa blusher!

BEAT THE CHAPS!

No guy'll wanna hold dry 'n' chapped hands!

Just remember, every time you

2.
Got a nose like a beetroot? Hide it with some green coloured cream!

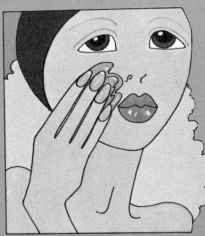

a clown! Failin' that, it could be one of two things. Either it's really cold, so warm it up with your mitts, or you've been blowin' your nose a lot, an' made it sore! Smooth in some cream, cos it'll be very dry, then get rid of the red with a little green coloured corrective cream! Yes, it really works!

DRY 'N' CRACKED!

Your lips are gettin' rough an' flaky-lookin' from the cold or is it that you've just been biting them?

Do somethin' quickly, cos no guy'll like kissin' those! Always wear lip salve, even under lipstick. It's colourless and really works!

Don't forget to carry your lip salve in your handbag, so that you can renew it. An' no more bitin' your lips! It'll make it worse!

CREEPY COLD SORES!

A great big cold sore has planted itself right on the side of your mouth, and it looks ridiculous!

Ooohh! They really hurt, an' there's not much you can do for 'em. They just come an' go when they please! If you're kinda prone an' you can feel one comin', see your Doctor right away, an' he'll give you somethin' for it. You can hide it with a spot stick, y'know. Watch it tho', cos they spread easily!

HOW TO KEEP WARM 'N' COSY!

Ol' Jack Frost is sneaky, so keep an eye out for him! He looks for anywhere that you haven't got covered and then he'll attack! So keep wrapped up! There are oodles of bright, woolly hats an' scarves around, so there's no excuse! Keep to layers, instead of wearin' one massive jumper—you'll soon feel how much warmer it is!

We dressed our model like that an' sent her out in the cold (booo... aren't we mean!) for her to tell us how she felt! Well, she came back shiverin' an' shakin' with her · teeth goin' ten-to-the-dozen! Foiled! . . . we thought! We'll give ourselves a kick up the bum for bein' wrong! An' then the sneaky rotter burst out laughing! She'd been warm all the time! You wanna know the secret? Well, it's a Marks & Spencer vest! Really! It'll keep you as warm as toast! Start with one of those, an' a thick pair of woolly socks. And add a silky pole, a pair of corduroy trousers tucked into wellies, a chunky sweater, an' a corduroy jacket! Phew! An', of course, not forgetting your woolly hat 'n' scarf an' gloves to match! Now you will be ready for anything! So when you see Jack learin' at ya, give him a punch on the nose for us. Will ya!!

MIKE'S SECRET FEARS

Looking at that cute innocent face and into those big honest eyes, you wouldn't think that Mike Holoway had a serious worry in the world. But Mike has secret fears that often keep him awake at night . . .

"I HAVE terrible nightmares sometimes about walking down the street and passing all my friends. They don't nod or say hello, they all just walk right past me as if I'm a stranger.

"That's something I am petrified *will* happen, that I really will lose all my mates. You're in a group, you start to travel around the country and suddenly you never seem to have the time for a night out any more and you're never at home when people call round for you.

"I'm used to having a lot of friends and I'd hate to lose them by becoming really famous. You don't have to ignore old mates just because you appear on TV a few times but I guess some of 'em get a bit jealous.

"When Flintlock started to appear in the series, 'You Must Be Joking', all the girls we knew went bonkers! Each morning we arrived at the 87 bus-stop and there'd be dozens of girls there too who wouldn't get on any bus except the one we were catchin'.

"That got a bit daft so we started cycling to school. An' it's funny cos all the fellas reacted in a completely opposite way. They ignored us mostly and when I talked to the rest of the group about it, they said it was probably just jealousy.

"Well, a few blokes I only vaguely knew didn't bother me but I hope that doesn't happen to any of my close mates.

"The truth is that I just want to stay an ordinary guy. If I am feelin' a bit low, I discuss things with my Mum and Dad. It helps a lot more than taking overdoses and getting desperate like the Rollers.

"Mum gets a bit upset at times about me being in show business. She doesn't really like it but she'd never say anything directly.

Dad's the one who's always been keen on the idea and given me a lot of encouragement. Mum's helped too of course but secretly I'm sure she'd rather I studied as a doctor or lawyer!

"I want to be successful at something and I'm a bit frightened myself that I'll end up a failure when I'm older. Quite a few people are said to be budding stars when they're young and then spend the rest of their lives wondering what happened or didn't happen.

"I'm going to try and be honest with myself so that doesn't happen to me. If my chance is now then I'm gonna take it and get out while the going's still good.

SCARRED

"Being in the kind of job that relies on your looks as well as your talent makes you a bit vain, I guess. Once when I came close to being involved in a car accident I remember thinking how awful it would have been if my face had got scarred. Not whether I might have been crippled, which is much worse really, but if my face would've been marked.

"An' this may sound really silly but I do wonder sometimes if I'm ever going to meet the right girl for me. If I do stay in the pop world, I can only see me meeting the kind of girl who'll want me because I'm famous.

"I don't want that sort of girl, the ones who want to be taken to flash places so that they can be seen with you. I'm looking for someone who'll love me for just being Mike Holoway, an ordinary fella from Dagenham. It *is* very frightening you know, the idea of bein' a star with no one you can really trust.

"As soon as your name reaches the papers, the hangers-on start to appear. The ones who think there's money to be made, or excitement to share if they can get near you.

"You've got to be so careful that you keep your feet on the ground. When photographers are ringing you up every week asking to take your picture, it's pretty difficult not to get carried away.

"As I've already said, my father gives me a lot of guidance but as a group, Flintlock do make a lot of their own decisions. Derek and the others seem to have a lot of confidence in the business side of things but I get petrified. After our first series we were offered a £50,000 advance by one record company. And we turned it down!

"Derek explained it to me, he's really smart at things like that. When he got a paper round to help out with money, he started his own little business. He bought eight rounds from newsagents and got other boys to do six of them for him! That's being clever.

"Anyway, he said it was better to get a shorter contract with a smaller company that'd take care of us. Then we wouldn't be tied for years on a fixed income. Lots of groups find themselves at the top of the charts and only earning £40 a week. Luckily, that's not going to happen to us.

"Basically I think we've been wise but you can't help having doubts. Maybe I'm just a born worrier, like my mother. She's the one who lies awake at night to listen out for us coming back from a gig. She can't sleep unless I'm safe indoors.

"If I make a million, retire to the country and live in a beautiful mansion, I'll still be worrying that the roof will fall in!"

PART 2

OH BOY! OH BOY! THEY'RE BEAUTIFUL!

Here are your second helpings in the Oh Boy! picture parade.

And if this still ain't enough for you, well, you'll just have to buy Oh Boy! every week—'cos we always feature the greatest-looking guys!

Meanwhile, have a good drool over this tasty bunch . . .

Same charm's there as his brother always had. Cheeky Shaun Cassidy is quite a bit like David. Impish an' always smilin', but deep inside thoughtful and serious. Nice clean hair and friendly face with natty clothes. Someone you'd be proud to be seen with, looks good, confident, smart.

Lovely Woody looks like a lost waif. Tufty locks an' mischievous grin tell you he's not an ordinary boy. He likes to laugh, pull jokes and play tricks. Not wild but just a bit wicked. Sweet too 'tho with a friendly face. Not quite handsome but more attractive because of it, his personality shows through . . .

Dennis Waterman, tough but not mean. The kinda guy who'd protect you in the dark and make you feel all cosy in his arms. He's a big brute but the nicest kind. If some villain tied you to a railway track, you'd just *know* Dennis would be there in time to save ya!

It's those big brown eyes of Alan Merrill's that make yer legs go all wobbly. That 'lost little boy' look which makes you wanna pick him up and take him home. Nice dark lashes, sweet button nose, cute cupid lips an' all! Best keep him out the way of your mum tho'—she'd wanna feed him up on bread 'n' broth.

He's used to speaking, Kid Jensen. That's why you can tell he's interesting, chatty, fun. You don't have to listen to the radio to know he's bound to have a nice voice. You can imagine it anyway. Nice body too, with fair hair right in the middle of his chest. Masculine but slim, enough to grab hold of!

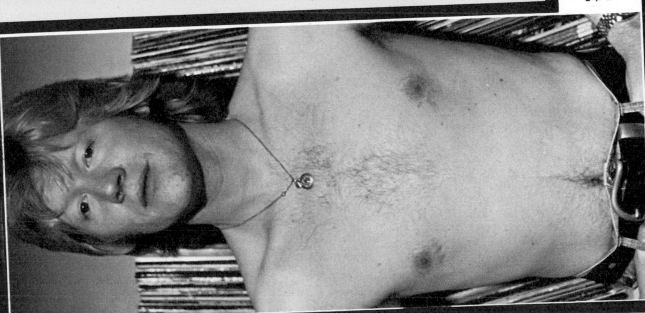

THEY'RE NOT BUMS

Our fave cowboys get a right pasting from that dust in the desert, y'know—they look like walking ant hills (an' that's nasty!) when they come off the set. But one episode Kurt and Tim really loved was when they spent the whole day in the tub. Any woman under 49 was banned from the set— and you could hear their faint cries outside all day!

The Baudine Boys settle down for a nice long soak . . . Tim's a little nervous tho' . . . last time he was in a tub with Kurt around he nearly got drowned in the fun. This time he's keeping his legs out, so he can spring away at the first sign of trouble (usually Kurt grinning evilly!).

No such worries for Kurt. He's an expert swimmer and kept ducking his head under water for minutes on end in case anybody didn't believe it. Kurt also didn't wear trunks like Tim had on, cos he said they 'chafed him to ribbons'. The producer began to realise just how wise he'd been banning young ladies from the set!

DIRTY LOWDOWN ANYMORE

Suddenly Kurt whipped out what he'd been hiding under the water —a massive six gun! "Oops, forgot to take the ol' gun belt off . . ." he giggled. "An' I do believe I've got my rifle under here too, and a couple of bison. Hey, Tim, you know what the difference is between a buffalo and a bison ?"

"Nope" said Tim, and it looked as if he didn't care much, either. "You can't wash your hands in a buffalo," came the reply. Tim just looked at Kurt for a long while—till he realised he'd got his paper all wet. Then he said a cowboy expression that was very rude indeed, and Kurt practically drowned himself laughing. Yep—bath time is laugh time with the Baudines!

NOW IT'S YOUR TURN TO JUMP IN! SEE OVER!

IT'S A

Fancy havin' a fun time? Well, take a bath! Lock yourself away where no-one will find you—and dive beneath the bubbles! It's a great time for practising whistlin', yodellin', or any other strange noises you wanna make! Cos there'll be nobody around to hear you!

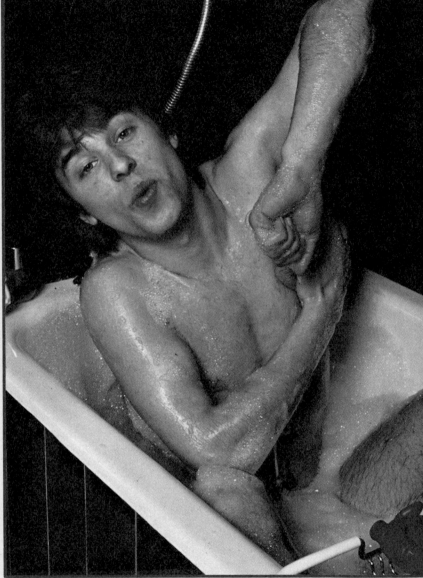

What you do in there is up to you, besides washing well, of course! But, it is a good opportunity to get your feet sparklin' clean, rubbin' any rough skin with a pumice stone, and to do a few footy exercises! You didn't know there were any, did you? There are! Pop one foot first above the bubbles, and slowly move your toes as if they are drawing a circle. Do this 10 times, then try the other one. It's good for the feet, 'cos they've been cramped up in tight shoes all day, and it gives 'em a breather!

Whilst you're in there, you may as well have a face pack. Try one of these fruity ones:

Green Apple Mask (for oily skin)

Grate a large, green apple and spread this all over your face. Wash off with

BATH A MINUTE!

warm water after 10 minutes.

Lemon Mask (for oily skin)

Add milk an' lemon juice to oatmeal (like Porridge Oats) that'll deep cleanse your skin. Leave on for 10 minutes, then rinse off with cold water.

Eggy Mask (for dry skin)

Separate the yolk from the white of the egg and mix it with a teaspoon of olive oil. Smooth it on your face and leave, again, for 10 minutes. Wash off in warm water and pat dry.

Rub away any hard patches of skin on your legs, elbows and back with a firm massage with a loofah or a soapy face flannel.

Dry really thoroughly, 'specially behind your knees, and then rub in lotsa body lotion or oil all over. Once that has 'soaked' in sprinkle yourself with talc and apply anti-perspirant as usual.

NO FUZZY-WUZZIES!

Now you're smellin' great an' feelin' soft, it's no good spoilin' it by havin' hairy legs an' armpits, is it? So a bit of de-fuzzin' is in order!

BLEACH 'EM

If the hair isn't very coarse and you just want to make it less obvious, then bleaching is your best bet. You can use this on your face, arms an' legs. Try a good product like Jolen Creme Bleach which you can find at most large chemists. It's expensive, but it lasts ages. Or make your own. Take 2 teaspoonsful of 10 vol. peroxide, 2 teaspoonsful of warm water, mixed with 1 teaspoonful of cloudy ammonia. Always do a patch test before using, in case you're allergic to it. Dab a little of the solution on your wrist, then rinse off with warm water. If there's no inflammation after 24 hours, you're okay!

SHAVE IT OFF!

This is a quick 'n' easy method for removing hair. The only drawback is that it grows back quickly, so once you start you have to keep it up!

PEACHES 'N' CREAM?

A good method for removing hair on your face, like a 'moustache', or from your legs, is what we call a depilatory cream. There are loads of brands around, some specifically for your face and others for your body, so watch out!

WAXWORKS!

Waxing removes hair at a deeper level than other methods. That's as long as you don't have sensitive skin tho'! 'Cos it's a little tricky to do, and when the wax dries you have to pull it off like a plaster! You can buy it at chemists, an' it is quite cheap.

ELECTROLYSIS

If you want to get rid of your fuzz for good, then this is the only way. The root of the hair is destroyed by a tiny electrical charge and you'll only feel a tingle! You can't do this yourself tho', so if you wanna list of professional people who do it, see your Doctor.

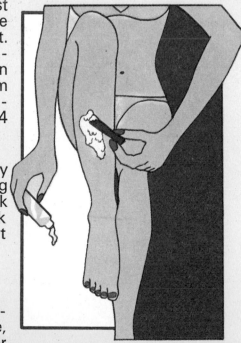

WHEN CHILD

We nearly had to leave when Child exploded onto the stage at

It was partly Graham's fault—he got so EXCITINGLY close!

SHEFFIELD Top Rank it was. The night Child went wild, and the crowd went daft. Steve went white and Nicki went a sort of khaki green which was definitely DEAD unfashionable!

We were there to witness the incredible effect these Yorkshire hoods can have on a crowd. They'd promised us the girls would go bananas—and they really did—whole bunches of 'em!

Tim and Keith play up the 'cheeky devils' image while Graham and David stay sort of free and cool—they know that there's a fair amount of girls that go for the quiet types too!

Halfway into their first number one fan managed to get herself caught up in Graham's guitar lead and for about 20 beautiful seconds she was entangled with the handsome hunk!

Later she was to go home and write a poem about it—and become the heroine of her local youth club. Now she just looked dazed, amazed, and the happiest fan in pop. She'd been caught up with a Child!

Tim and Keith share a funny before the show. Then they're into the Atack!

WENT WILD!

Sheffield last summer. Things just got TOO HOT!

Tim didn't help either! When he blew a kiss the arms went out like this!

The famous nudie pic that started it all. Just think—one lucky Oh Boy reader owns a huge signed copy of it, from the Bonanza!

That really seemed to set the crowd off. They made desperate lunges and managed to make their arms stretch yards to touch the boys. But Child stayed just that painful inch out of reach—playing the sort of heavy rock that would make Gran's teeth shoot out of her mouth at 80 mph!

Steve and Nicki by this time were clutching each other for comfort (well, that was their story!) and dodging the suicide rushes of the fans. It was worse than knocking-off time at the office!

Then, after an ear-spattering drum solo from Keith, followed by boggling bass and lead runs from the others, everything suddenly went deathly quiet. The lights flicked off, and the boys were gone.

The silence lasted for a second, then a wail went up . . . a heart rending moan of a wail that filled the whole hall. A thousand eyes were pricked with tears, and the hands still reached out—towards the darkness.

Another Child concert was over.

GRAHAM—FOR GETTING UP IN TIME!

Yes—the sleepiest Child of all actually got up on time and arrived for his interview with Steve two minutes early! Steve was so surprised he nearly swallowed his notepad! And thanks for being one of our world-famed Oh Boy good-lookers, Graham—we need as many of you as we can get!

WOODY—FOR KEEPING US WARM!

Woody, thanks a bomb! You kept our pulses whizzing last winter with that nudie (plus giant scarf!) pic—you must've been frozen solid doing it, but it's as good as a wall heater on the notice board near where the Oh Boy birds sit!